THE U.S. NAVAL INSTITUTE ON

MILITARY JUSTICE

U.S. NAVAL INSTITUTE
WHEEL BOOKS

In the U.S. Navy, "Wheel Books" were once found in the uniform pockets of every junior and many senior petty officers. Each small notebook was unique to the Sailor carrying it, but all had in common a collection of data and wisdom that the individual deemed useful in the effective execution of his or her duties. Often used as a substitute for experience among neophytes and as a portable library of reference information for more experienced personnel, those weathered pages contained everything from the time of the next tide, to leadership hints from a respected chief petty officer, to the color coding of the phone-and-distance line used in underway replenishments.

In that same tradition, U.S. Naval Institute Wheel Books provide supplemental information, pragmatic advice, and cogent analysis on topics important to all naval professionals. Drawn from the U.S. Naval Institute's vast archives, the series combines articles from the Institute's flagship publication *Proceedings*, as well as selections from the oral history collection and from Naval Institute Press books, to create unique guides on a wide array of fundamental professional subjects.

THE U.S. NAVAL INSTITUTE ON
MILITARY JUSTICE

EDITED BY CHRIS BRAY

NAVAL INSTITUTE PRESS
Annapolis, Maryland

Naval Institute Press
291 Wood Road
Annapolis, MD 21402

Library of Congress Cataloging-in-Publication Data
Names: Bray, Chris (Historian), author. | United States Naval Institute.
Title: The U.S. Naval Institute on military justice / Chris Bray.
Other titles: US Naval Institute on military justice | United States Naval
    Institute on military justice
Description: Annapolis, Maryland : Naval Institute Press, [2018] |
    Series: U.S. Naval Institute Wheel Books | Includes index.
Identifiers: LCCN 2017049558 | ISBN 9781682471487 (pbk. : alk. paper)
Subjects: LCSH: Courts-martial and courts of inquiry—United States. |
    Naval law—United States.
Classification: LCC KF7650 .B73 2018 | DDC 343.730143—dc23
    LC record available at https://lccn.loc.gov/2017049558

26 25 24 23 22 21 20 19 18   9 8 7 6 5 4 3 2 1
First printing

CONTENTS

EDITOR'S NOTE

This book is an anthology, compiled from work written in different centuries, by differing standards, and with different values. I have mostly left the style of each selection intact, to occasionally quirky effect. My intent is to let readers encounter each of the excerpted works more or less as they were written, preserving their unique tone. This means that a reader will sometimes come across unusual punctuation, odd phrasing, and awkward grammar. With the exception of some obvious spelling and typesetting mistakes, I have not corrected these selections. You read them more or less as they first appeared.

Encountering texts from the nineteenth and early twentieth century just as they were written, readers will notice anachronistic language about gender. In these excerpts from historical articles and books, writers mostly talk about the challenges for naval officers as they disciplined their men. Reflecting my intention to present these pieces as they were first published, I have not changed language about gender to reflect the current realities of a Navy that includes women, trusting that readers will approach these selections with an understanding of when they were written. We have changed; the past has not.

The most significant change I have made to these texts is to shorten many of them, cutting out repetitive and extraneous material so a reader can get right to the substance of each selection. Where a writer offered five examples to make a point that is clear with three examples, I provide three of the originally published examples. So that you can tell where I have edited a selection, ellipses appearing in the original text appear without brackets; ellipses that indicate my cuts are bracketed: [...].

I have also removed all citations in every selection that included them. This anthology is meant as a general set of introductory readings, not as scholarly work. The original articles and books are easily found, with citations intact.

In fact, my first hope is that readers who find these selections interesting and valuable will pursue further reading in them. With the exception of a handful of unpublished oral histories, this is a collection of excerpts from published work. Many articles excerpted here are from U.S. Naval Institute *Proceedings* and can be read online by Naval Institute members. Some are from Naval Institute Press books that merit a close reading, such as James E. Valle's magnificent 1980 book, *Rocks and Shoals: Order and Discipline in the Old Navy, 1800–1861*. In more than one case, I hope the excerpted pages published here will convince some readers to dive into the whole book or essay.

A last note: In the excerpted articles that follow, bylines indicate the rank of military writers at the time of publication, as given in the excerpted pieces.

INTRODUCTION

Military justice is harsh, capricious, and grotesquely unfair. Or it is sensible, rational, and paternal, administered carefully by officers who care deeply about the people who serve under their care.

Both of these opinions, and many others in the middle ground between them, have been expressed with equal confidence by people inside and outside of the U.S. armed forces. The selections that follow were chosen with an eye toward a diversity of experience and opinion. They include voices that, for example, lament the implementation of the Uniform Code of Military Justice for its unforgivable civilianization of military justice, and they include the voices of people who think the UCMJ didn't go far enough in creating lawyer-run martial justice.

Seeking a diverse range of voices, I have also looked for selections from a long range of American naval history. The pieces that follow are presented in largely chronological order, though some cover more than one moment. Some discuss a single court-martial; many offer a broader discussion of military law and of military justice as a system. All are relevant to a reader trying to understand how we arrived at the naval justice of today, after the debates and failures of the past.

Through all the disagreements and arguments that have characterized the American discussion of military justice, a few widely shared themes have persisted, and they echo through these selections of historical material.

First, justice and discipline are wholly a part of the total ethos of command. Bad leaders punish badly, and their subordinates know it; good leaders punish with wisdom, and people notice. Favoritism in discipline devastates the trust that must exist between a commander and his subordinates in a healthy military organization. An officer who administers unequal justice is discredited as a leader. That was true under our older system of naval justice, and it is true under the UCMJ. A leader trying to find the right balance in 1800 still has something to say to a contemporary naval officer.

Second, courts-martial have too often been politicized, especially in the case of high-profile controversies. Military charges have been tools in factional conflicts and power struggles, particularly in the early Navy and Marine Corps. Naval leaders have struck at their institutional opponents by filing charges, and some courts have been stacked with members of a particular faction. Though most courts-martial have not been infected by political maneuvering, some have been. Military justice can be politics by other means.

Taking the first point and the second point together, the politicization of courts-martial is harmful to the morale and cohesion of military organizations. If military justice can be politics by other means, it should not be.

Third, change in the world outside the court-martial reaches deeply into the world of the military courtroom. World War II and the Vietnam War shook the military justice system; big wars have led to big arguments about the way members of the armed forces are brought to justice, particularly as the armed forces have filled up with conscripts and short-term, noncareer volunteers. Sudden changes in the composition of military organizations cause sudden changes in the way discipline works in the ranks. During the two major world wars of the twentieth century, military leaders discovered that many of the new soldiers and sailors they led did not regard a bad conduct discharge as a punishment; instead, they celebrated being thrown out of the military as an escape. How do you discipline people who have wildly divergent ideals of honor and disparate attitudes about the very idea of military service?

Finally, in a bigger restatement of the point about individual commanders, the most important point these selections make about military justice is that *culture matters*. Proud, able, well-led armed forces are more likely to manage the problems of discipline and justice well. The health of the Navy and the health of Navy courts-martial are firmly linked.

In this last point, I confess my own bias: While military justice reformers argue, above all, for the importance of law and lawyers in making the court-martial fair and effective, I think they point in the wrong direction. A commander whose decisions are animated by a sense of honor and fairness, leading proud subordinates, is the strongest foundation of honest military justice. Good culture, good justice.

But the selections in this anthology will not all make that point, and I hope you will find many points of view represented in the pages that follow.

1 "BASES OF NAVAL LAW"

CAPT Roger E. Nelson, USN

In an essay first published in March of 1949, a Naval Academy graduate lays out the most basic foundations of naval law. In a Navy that was more than 150 years old, Captain Nelson decided to go back to the beginning to explain the present. The timing wasn't an accident: *Proceedings* published a study of the foundations of naval justice at the moment that Congress, still enmeshed in the controversies that arose from World War II courts-martial, was debating the changes that would usher in the Uniform Code of Military Justice.

"BASES OF NAVAL LAW"

By CAPT Roger E. Nelson, USN, U.S. Naval Institute *Proceedings* (March 1949): 269–77.

[. . .] It frequently happens that a bluejacket's first and most lasting impression of Naval Law is received something in this wise: The ship is headed South. It has left the cold winds of the North Atlantic and has entered the blue seas of the tropics. It is Saturday morning. The crew is mustered by divisions on the weather decks. The Captain and his heads of departments, having finished the long passage through the ranks of men, are inspecting the quarters below. The crew is in ranks at ease. On top of the turret stands an officer who holds before him at arm's length a large sheet of heavy paper from which he is reading aloud. His words, continually whipped away by the trade winds and confused in the swish of the waves, reach the men only in fragments of phrases: ". . . shall be punished as a court martial may adjudge . . . deserts in time of war . . . makes reproachful words or gestures . . . fails to do his utmost . . . strikes or attempts to strike the flag, or treacherously yields, or pusillanimously cries for quarter . . . punishment of death . . . sleeps upon his watch. . . ." That officer is publishing the Articles for the Government of the Navy to the crew. Heard so, they leave a vague memory of the promise of copious punishment, a long threat, a taste of blood and iron.

Now the Articles for the Government of the Navy are a Congressional statute. The reason the officer is upon the turret singing them out in the trade winds is precisely because one of their provisions requires that they shall be read once a month to the ship's company. Congressional statutes are public laws and any law must have, as the expression goes, "teeth in it," in order to be enforceable. Teeth there certainly are in the Articles! Usually it is the impression of the teeth which is retained from hearing them read, but actually the Articles are as much protective as punitive.

Why were the Articles enacted? Just how are they protective? To answer these questions it is helpful to go back to the Constitution, that instrument of ultimate competent authority which you have solemnly sworn to support and defend. The purpose which the people of the United States had in mind in adopting the Constitution is clearly expressed in its preamble: "We, the people of the United States, in order to form a more perfect Union, establish Justice, insure domestic Tranquility, provide for the common defence, promote the general welfare and secure the Blessings of Liberty to ourselves and our Posterity, do ordain and establish this Constitution for the United States of America." [. . .]

It is most significant that the people specifically reserved to Congress the authority to make rules for the government and regulation of the land and naval forces, an authority which now implicitly extends to air forces. This is a wise and protective measure for it insures that only a Congressional statute can govern the military forces—a congressional statute being, of course, subject to review by the Supreme Court. It therefore becomes impossible for the executive legally to take into its own hands the prescription of punitive measures in the armed forces. In consequence, the military services are protected against summary or severe punishment at the whim of any single individual.

By Article 6, paragraph 2, the people have established that: "This Constitution, and the Laws of the United States which shall be made in pursuance thereof . . . shall be the supreme Law of the Land." Quotation of this article may be redundant, but it serves to underscore the fact that the Articles for the Government of the Navy, enacted by Congress in accordance with the wish of the people, necessarily constitute supreme law in the Navy. It follows that any action by any commanding officer, or any court, or any executive authority, which is repugnant to the Constitution or to the Articles for the Government of the Navy is without legal basis; it cannot be approved or supported.

During the contest for the adoption of the Constitution, it developed that large numbers of people were not satisfied with the degree of personal liberty guaranteed by the instrument as originally written. This led to the adoption of the first ten amendments commonly known as the Bill of Rights. The organization and operation of a military service require a degree of regimentation and subordination on the part of each individual beyond that demanded or expected of a civilian. The military man does not enjoy individual freedom of action to the extent promised in the Bill of Rights. In general, this is well understood although non-professional soldiers chafe under it and have on occasion made considerable disturbance about it. Nevertheless a scrutiny of the Articles for the Government of the Navy will reveal the considerable extent to which the protections of the Bill of Rights have been carried into the basic law governing the Navy.

In this connection an excerpt from a report of the Committee of the Senate, which recently was studying the need for changes in the Articles of War and in the Articles for the Government of the Navy, is most instructive. The report says in part:

When the Congress in the early days of the Republic took up the question of establishing a system of military justice for the Army, John Adams and Thomas Jefferson stated that there was extant one system of Articles of War which had carried two Empires, the Roman and the British, to the head of mankind. They decided that it would be vain for them to seek in their own inventions or in the records of war-like nations for a more complete system of military justice and discipline. On their recommendations, the Congress adopted the Roman and British notions on this matter. As a result, the system of military justice in effect in the United States at the present time is an evolution of the laws of Caesar, just as the present system of American civil justice has evolved from the principles enunciated in the British and Roman laws as developed through the centuries.

At the time these original notions were enacted into law by the American Congress, it was pointed out that the objective of an Army was wholly different from the objective of a civilian society; that the objective of military law differs from that of civilian law. These objectives were stated to be as wide apart as the poles, with each requiring its own separate system of laws. The function of an army, of a military organization, was then, as it remains today, not only to fight wars, but to win them. It is an organization which sends men obediently to their death, and which is designed for only that purpose. It is a collection of armed men obliged to obey one man. It is a hierarchy, and the men at the bottom cannot be treated or regarded as the military equals of those at the top, whatever their individual qualifications. This fundamental tenet was the basis of the rules governing the legions of Caesar, Charles Martel, Napoleon, and Pershing. And it was the governing factor in the control of the armies of Patton and Montgomery, the fleets of Nimitz and Cunningham, and the air forces of Spaatz and Tedder.

The difference between a military and a civilian organization was recognized in the fifth amendment of the Constitution, which specifically excepts from its guaranty of indictment by a grand jury cases arising in the land and naval forces. By judicial interpretation the same exception has been held applicable to the guaranty of jury trial recognized in the 6th amendment. This exception was considered so obvious by the founding fathers that it did not call forth a single word of discussion as it passed through the first session of the First Congress.

In the light of these remarks a brief review of the Articles to see what they have to say and what in general they accomplish will have interest. In addition to others less important, the Articles for the Government of the Navy accomplish the following specific things:

(a) They set up the authority of the chain of command
(b) They outline a penal code for the Navy
(c) Having established the penal code, they set up specific judicial procedures for its execution under which:
  (1) They prescribe the precise composition of naval courts-martial
  (2) They prescribe the means of convening naval courts-martial
  (3) They prescribe the review that shall be had of their proceedings
  (4) They specifically set up the extent and limitations of their power
  (5) In limited detail they prescribe how their proceedings shall be conducted
  (6) To some extent they prescribe how sentences shall be executed. [. . .]

[. . .] In a military service, because of its nature and purpose, some acts of lesser effect in civilian life must be regarded as offenses in military life. The Articles for the Government of the Navy provide a reasonable code of natural and naval offenses and the means of punishment for them. It is interesting to note that in writing these the First Congress considered twenty individual offenses sufficiently serious to name them specifically and to prescribe for them the punishment of death. The punishment of death is not made mandatory, but these specified offenses do find the word "death" mentioned in connection with them. They are to be found in Article 4. Two other offenses, namely murder, and spying or seduction to betrayal of trust, are considered worthy of the punishment of death and each has a separate article devoted to it, attesting its importance in the view of the legislators. Then about twenty-two additional offenses were considered by the First Congress to be of sufficient gravity to warrant specific mention as punishable, but in their cases, not by death. The words used here in Article 8 are "such punishment as a court-martial may adjudge." The Articles have a deal to say also about frauds against the Government, false musters and the like; and finally, recognizing that a penal code of this sort is not perfect, in Article 22 it is prescribed that "All offenses committed by persons belonging to the Navy which are not specified in the foregoing articles shall be punished as a court-martial shall direct."

It would be interesting to examine the Articles further in connection with punishment, but such examination would lead to a long analysis and would not necessarily serve our purposes. In very few cases does the Congress specify the exact punishment for an offense, preferring to leave it rather to the judgement of the prescribed court-martial; but for some reason the Congress singled out the officer who without leave absents himself from his command, and prescribed his punishment to be reduction to the rating of seaman second class.

The Establishment of Naval Courts-Martial

Having set up a penal code, the Articles then established the courts before which offenders are to be tried. The special nature of naval courts-martial should here be clearly understood. They are established by Federal statute specifically to try offenses under a penal code established by the same statute; they are therefore Federal Courts. Moreover, they are Federal Criminal Courts because their jurisdiction extends only to offenses against the penal code set up by the statute. This means that they are Federal Criminal Courts of limited jurisdiction. Since they are competent to try only criminal cases, and further only criminal cases arising from breach of the Articles, they are subject to the following limitations:

(a) They are limited as to the *person* they may try—he must be a member of the Naval service to be amenable to trial by a naval court-martial

(b) They are limited as to the *offense* they may try—for it must be an offense specified in the Articles

(c) They are limited as to the *place*; that is, the offense must have been committed within the jurisdictional authority of the Navy, else it cannot be brought before a naval court-martial

(d) They are limited as to *time*—for the offense must have been committed while the offender was a member of the naval service

(e) Finally, they are limited by the Articles in many cases as to the *extent of punishment* which they may adjudge. [. . .]

We have seen how the Articles rest in the Constitution, and how they set up the Navy's penal code and chain of command. Now what about Regulations, orders, and instructions? By appealing once more to the Constitution, we find that in Article II, Section 2(1) of the Constitution the people have said: "The President shall be the Commander-in-Chief of the Army and Navy of the United States . . . and he shall have power to grant Reprieves and Pardons for offenses against the United States, except in cases of Impeachment."

Hence the President, as Constitutional Commander-in-Chief, is the competent authority from which originate the lawful orders for operation of the naval service. This authority extends down through the Secretary of Defense, the Secretary of the Navy, and on down the chain of command. Orders of a permanent nature are brought together and published as the *Navy Regulations*, *Naval Courts and Boards*, the manuals of the various Bureaus of the Navy Department, the *Fleet Tactical Instructions*, and so on. By this process these publications become a written source of naval law, part of the body of rules prescribed by competent authority. Their requirements must be carried out, and willful failure or disobedience are punishable by the penal code.

It is noteworthy, in view of what has gone before, that the *Navy Regulations* go into considerable detail as to how the investigations preceding a court-martial are to be carried out. *Naval Courts and Boards* goes into considerable detail in setting forth the rights and privileges of the accused, the rules of evidence, and the manner in which courts-martial are to arrive at their decisions.

Such are the written sources of naval law. *Courts and Boards* tells us that there are four unwritten sources as well, namely: (a) Decisions of the courts; (b)

Decisions of the President and the Secretary of the Navy, and Opinions of the Attorney General and Judge-Advocate General of the Navy; (c) Court-martial orders; (d) Customs and usages of the service. Of these the first three are in fact written in the sense that they are in published form and available for reference. The difference is that they are not legal enactments but rather authoritative interpretations of questions. [. . .]

The final unwritten sources of Naval Law we have been given consist of customs and usages of the service. To become a competent authority in the terms of Naval law, a custom must be very firmly established. In fact, it has to satisfy seven conditions: namely, it must be (1) long continued, (2) certain and uniform, (3) compulsory, (4) consistent, (5) general, (6) well known, (7) not in opposition to a lawful regulation. Custom and usage are in some degree synonymous. But a usage must be long continued and must satisfy the six other requirements given before it can be considered a custom. This is a rather extensive field and one difficult to delimit. Many of the offenses charged under Article 24 of the Articles for the Government of the Navy must be appealed to custom. This article says, "All offenses committed by persons belonging to the Navy which are not specified in the foregoing articles shall be punishable as a court-martial may direct."

Examples of Navy custom, some of which have actually been finally incorporated in regulations or orders, are the salute to the quarter deck when boarding a man-of-war, the old tradition of piping the side, or the privilege of sitting in the stern seats reserved to the senior officers embarked in a boat.

Naval law, customs, traditions, courtesies are all warp and weft of one fabric. Captain Hopwood, R.N., has given a sound admonition in his poem:

> Now these are the laws of the Navy,
> Unwritten and varied they be;
> And he that is wise will observe them
> Going down in his ship to the sea!

2 "ROCKS AND SHOALS"

(Selection from the introduction and chapters 1, 2, and 3 of *Rocks and Shoals*)

James E. Valle

In an important study of early U.S. naval justice, a history professor dug deeply into the archives to describe a system he compared to a "blind lottery."

"ROCKS AND SHOALS"

(Selection from the introduction and chapters 1, 2, and 3 of *Rocks and Shoals: Order and Discipline in the Old Navy, 1806–1861*) by James E. Valle (Naval Institute Press, 1980): 1–64.

[. . .] The general state of discipline in the nineteenth-century navy was discussed in letters, diaries, books, pamphlets, and even novels. Congressional committees made inquiries and conducted investigations; and various secretaries of the navy wrote reports and made recommendations, as each one in his turn wrestled with the tightly ingrained naval establishment of the early Republic.

The picture that emerges from these sources is engrossing and highly instructive. The Old Navy was, like most military organizations of that day, an authoritarian system based on the principle of dominance and domination. It was characterized by organizational rigidity and sought solutions for disciplinary problems through the mechanical application of traditional practices and routine policies. As were many other institutions of the time, it was noteworthy for its strong reliance on ceremonialism, conventional gestures, and formal observances that were built into its structure out of veneration for tradition and nostalgia. Its officers were, in conformity with the conventional culture from which they sprang, susceptible to an exaggerated sense of professionalism where concern with the forms and symbols of status outweighed regard for practical results and functional performance.

Out of this atmosphere there developed a curious quality of inconsistency characterized by a code of iron discipline which imposed the strictest possible control over the enlisted men. Because they were seen as the lowest class of humanity, reliance was placed mainly on flogging, confinement in irons, and the threat of capital punishment, on the grounds that that was all they could be expected to comprehend. Junior officers were under somewhat looser control. They could usually evade being punished for offenses that would send an enlisted man to the gratings; but let them incur the wrath of a senior officer, and they might find themselves summarily dismissed from the service or living under a regimen of petty harassment designed to elicit a resignation. Senior officers were somehow immune to most disciplinary restraints. They could feud, split the service with their factionalism, bend or break regulations, and indulge in highly autocratic behavior with little threat of serious reprisal. There was a great deal of favoritism about the way the navy administered justice, and the general public occasionally detected this and criticized the service for these habits. [...]

Enforcement of marine discipline was in the hands of the officer corps of the navy and its justice system when marines stationed aboard ship were accused of offenses. For this reason, the trials and punishments of marine officers and enlisted men are an integral part of the navy's records and statistics on courts-martial and courts of inquiry. Marines sailed and fought under the same Articles of War as naval men, committed essentially the same misdeeds, and were punished in the same ways.

When Richard Rush sailed for England in 1817 in the ship of the line *Franklin* to take up his post as minister to the Court of St. James, he was impressed by the excellent discipline and quiet efficiency of the crew. The marines presented a complete contrast. In conversation with Commodore Charles Stewart, the *Franklin*'s commanding officer, Rush learned that it was customary to keep well-trained and disciplined marines at home for ceremonial purposes and to send the raw recruits to sea. It took a great deal of effort, Stewart declared, within the confines of a ship to instill discipline in and teach close-order drill to men who had been only a few days in service before reporting aboard and who were, at best, the dregs of society. However much this generalization may or may not have applied to the marines afloat, the corps is certainly well represented on the punishment rolls and in the records of courts-martial. Nineteen percent of all cases in the judge advocate general's records index for the years 1800 to 1861 involve marines. They also account for 30 percent of all death sentences handed down by naval courts. [...]

[...] "An Act for the Better Government of the Unites States Navy" was passed on 23 April 1800. This act, consisting of [John] Adams's first Articles of War plus the changes desired by the Federalist-controlled Congress, has been referred to variously as the Articles of War of 1800, the Act for the Government of the Navy, the Act of 1800, or simply the Articles of War. It is the code that generations of naval men have nicknamed "Rocks and Shoals," and it remained in force with a few modifications until replaced in 1950 by the Uniform Code of Military Justice. [...]

As the first captain to command a major ship in the Federal Navy, Thomas Truxtun was highly conscious of the fact that he was setting an example for his subordinate officers and establishing precedents that would long be perpetuated in the service. He worked hard to create an atmosphere of total subordination and reflexive obedience because he believed that this was the style of discipline that would yield the best results in battle and that all other considerations were secondary to success in action. He strove to make his ship and crew a perfect instrument of his will, issuing detailed instructions to his officers prescribing their conduct in a variety of situations. No officer was to offer an opinion on the working of the ship unless requested to do so. No officer was to sleep on shore without his permission. Officers must be civil "and polite to every one and par-ticularly so to strangers, for civility does not interfere with discipline: To obey without hesitation is a maxim always practiced by me to my superiors in every point of duty and the same sort of conduct I expect in return by all officers under my orders."

Officers were further enjoined to avoid becoming too familiar with their men and warned to eschew "that detestable vice, drunkenness . . ."

Truxtun's austere example made a vivid impression on Lieutenant John Rodgers, who, when he attained his own command, elaborated further on the scheme and created the "Rodgers System" of maintaining order, which was copied throughout the service. Seeking to keep crews healthy, under good discipline, and hard at work, the Rodgers system called for an absolute minimum of shore liberty, a constant round of "busy work," and judicious use of corporal punishment. Rodgers himself was a popular commander who found it necessary to flog his men only in unusual circumstances. When he commanded the Mediterranean Squadron, 1825–1828, only thirteen floggings were logged in his flagship *North Carolina* in two years. Since the *North Carolina* was a ship of the line with almost a thousand men on board, this record is impressive. Frigates and sloops of war with half as many men often saw a half-dozen floggings in a single week. [. . .]

[. . .] The common sailors of the Old Navy were representative of the lower orders of society in a day and age when class differences were much more pronounced. Since the earliest days of the British sea service, the officer corps had regarded the foremast hands as the dregs of society and worse—as criminals, cutthroats, and potential mutineers. American naval officers were no different; in fact, lines were even more sharply drawn in the ships and squadrons of republican America. The American enlisted man had no entrée into the society of congressmen and bureaucrats. There was no prominent personage to manage his appointment or keep a friendly eye on his naval career. When he was brought before the bar of naval justice, his crimes and offenses were often different in nature from those of the officers and not often conducive to eliciting sympathy. Punishments meted out to enlisted men were not publicized, usually took place out of the public eye, and were administered so quickly that any campaign on the part of the sailor to secure "vindication" or reversal of a verdict was pointless. It was in dealing with the enlisted men on the subjudicial level that the naval justice system actually displayed the uncompromising and arbitrary character of the Roman-British codes.

There were, however, factors at work which tended to mitigate the harshness of naval discipline even for the lowly sailor. [Herman] Melville wrongly believed that no American seaman was ever flogged 'round the fleet in an American port because naval officers feared that such a spectacle would infuriate the civilian populace and cause a riot. Likewise, in 1800 at Norfolk, when a court-martial on board the frigate *Congress* convicted several seamen of mutiny and sentenced two of them to be hanged, Commodore Thomas Truxtun mitigated the punishments to one hundred lashes and dismissal from the service in order to spare the civilian population the sight of American seamen dangling from the yardarms of a public vessel. Nearly all death sentences conferred by naval courts-martial involved enlisted men, but most of them were commuted by the President to prison terms at hard labor. In the three certain instances where American seamen were executed by the Navy, two occurred on stations so remote from Washington that presidential intervention was impractical, and one case, the hanging of the *Somers* mutineers [*Editor's note:* discussed in a later chapter], involved the execution of three men at sea by a captain who had become convinced that he had to act to save his ship. Obviously, the force of public opinion was something that the naval justice system had to take into account in its treatment of enlisted men.

The political system also contained persons who were interested in humanizing American naval justice. By the decade of the 1840s, the United States contained reform movements dedicated to a variety of causes ranging from the treatment of prisoners and inmates of insane asylums to the abolition of slavery. The drive to improve the condition of the Navy's enlisted men became part of this movement and spawned, among other things, a powerful movement to abolish flogging as a means of punishment.

In many ways flogging was a natural target for reformers. It was common in almost all American men-of-war, a cruel and revolting thing to witness, and it invariably resulted in at least the temporary disabling of any person undergoing it. In addition, the practice seemed repugnant to America's republican ideology and democratic notions of the dignity of the individual. Civilian government officials taking passage in navy ships became incensed at the continual round of floggings they witnessed, and occasionally an eloquent denunciation or a particularly graphic description of the practice was penned by an articulate sailor and gained wide circulation among the reading public.

By 1850, the movement to abolish flogging in the navy had achieved the status of a *cause celebre*, pitting congressional and humanitarian reformers against the officer corps and their allies in conservative political circles. The reformers eventually scored a victory, and the abolition of flogging became the greatest single change to occur in the navy's treatment of enlisted men until the twentieth century.

Other attempts to reform the navy's justice system were far less successful in the decades prior to the Civil War and centered mostly on the *Naval Regulations*, a body of written articles which supplemented the Articles of War and regulated such routine practices as the issuing of food and liquor rations, the duties of officers and petty officers, the outfitting of ships, and other aspects of service life.

The first set of regulations put into force in the Federal Navy were issued by President Adams in 1798 and bore the title *Marine Rules and Regulations*. This compendium included 116 articles and was supplemented by sets of internal regulations composed and enforced by individual commanding officers. In 1801, President Jefferson's Secretary of the Navy, Robert Smith, recommended that a new set of regulations be drafted. These rules were composed by the Department and circulated among those of the navy's senior captains who were then residing ashore or stationed in home waters. John Barry, Thomas Truxtun, Richard Morris, and Alexander Murray reviewed the proposals in turn and added their comments and additions. The resulting document was printed and issued to the fleet under the title of *Naval Regulations 1802*.

By 1815 the *Naval Regulations*, which now consisted of 194 articles and had come to be known colloquially as the Black Book, were widely recognized to be in need of revision. They included numerous British codes originally copied by Adams, acts of the long defunct Continental Congress, and additions inserted by the legislative and executive branches after 1798. Many of them were loosely worded and prolix enough to cause endless confusion. For example, article 10 in the section entitled "Of the Duties of a Captain or Commander" reads as follows:

> 10. As, from the beginning of the campaign, the plan of combat ought to be formed, he shall have his directions given, and his people so placed, as to not be unprovided against any accident which may happen.

The first Board of Naval Commissioners, consisting of Commodores John Rodgers, David Porter, and Stephen Decatur, spent much of its time revising and clarifying these rules; and their work was circulated to the Navy in 1818 in the form of a new set of rules and regulations known as the Blue Book. The result was less than satisfactory. The old regulations, whatever their faults, had been legally approved by Congress and thus had the force of law behind them. The Blue Book, not having congressional approval, was technically illegal in any instance where its provisions contradicted those of the Black Book, so the Navy Department was obliged to follow the Blue Book into circulation with a general order annulling large parts of it because they set aside acts of Congress which had never been repealed.

In 1832 a second attempt was made to reform the regulations, which now consisted of the Blue Book and its modifying circular and portions of the Black Book. A board of senior captains was constituted and produced the Red Book, the contents of which set off a storm of controversy in the navy because the board neglected to provide any limits on the power of prerogatives of commodores and senior captains. The protests of younger captains and junior officers were so vigorous that the Red Book was never fully adopted, leaving the Navy with a confused and almost unworkable tangle of contradictory documents that were its rules and regulations. [. . .]

Secretary [James] Paulding made an attempt to rectify this state of affairs in 1840 or 1841. He had an entirely new set of rules and regulations, consisting of nearly eight hundred articles, drawn up and circulated. This document was not the work of an official naval board. In fact, the officers of the navy were mystified as to just exactly who had authored them, but repeated inquiries about them addressed to the Department went unanswered. No congressional approval was ever sought for Paulding's rules, but some of them, presumably those which did not contradict previous legislation, were put into effect in the service. [...]

The chaotic condition of the rules and regulations was not due entirely to the stupidity of various secretaries of the navy nor was it attributable entirely to a lack of managerial skills on the part of the officer corps. It was symptomatic of a much deeper problem which was manifested in Congress and rooted in the nation at large. In all truth, there was no consensus in America on the subject of naval discipline. Southerners and Federalists had framed the Articles of War and the navy's first regulations in order to fulfill ideological needs of their own. During the decades after 1815, the North, having shed Federalism, began to move towards a more liberal and egalitarian view of society and towards more enlightened methods of social control. As the sectional and ideological dispute between the North and South grew deeper and more heated, the question of naval discipline and its reform became a small part of the larger struggle. The Southerners perceived that a liberalization or humanization of naval discipline would give aid and comfort to those forces which opposed the flogging of slaves and the draconian treatment meted out to runaway bondsmen. Northerners felt that if they could liberalize military discipline, it would have the effect of leaving the Southern slaveholders standing in embarrassed isolation as the last remaining practitioners of flogging and arbitrary justice in general.

3 "YOU KNOW HE IS NOT A MAN WHO COMMANDS HIS TEMPER"

(Selection from chapter 12 of *Edward Preble*)

Christopher McKee

The early Navy officer Thomas Truxtun wrote that a warship was occupied by some "honest sailors," but among those were inevitably "a crew of abandoned miscreants, ripe for any mischief or villainy . . . and only deterred from the commission of any crime by the terror of severe punishment." Here, a distinguished naval historian describes the degree to which other early U.S. Navy officers agreed with Truxtun's ideas about justice for the men under his command. This selection is from the chapter on the period from August 1803 to February 1805.

"YOU KNOW HE IS NOT A MAN WHO COMMANDS HIS TEMPER"

(Selection from chapter 12 of *Edward Preble: A Naval Biography, 1761–1807*) by Christopher McKee (Naval Institute Press, 1996): 221–26.

[. . .]

Truxtun's convictions about the foundations of discipline in a ship of war were shared by almost all naval officers of Preble's day: most members of a ship's crew were inclined to good behavior, but there was always a hard core of dedicated troublemakers, if not criminals. A somewhat larger group of men was just as ready for mischief as was the hard core, but was deterred from breaking the rules by fear of severe punishment. The criminal element could corrupt the behavior of the entire crew. Strict discipline was the only way to hold these unruly forces under control. Although Preble never had much of a theoretical nature to say about discipline, his practice shows that he, too, shared these convictions: to maintain discipline he relied about equally on two punishments—confinement in irons and flogging.

On an average day in the *Constitution*, Master-at-Arms John Burchard would have under his charge two or three men in irons. Sometimes the number would be as low as one or as high as eight. More men were confined for drunkenness than for any other single violation. One particular morning found seven members of the *Constitution*'s Marine detachment in irons, sobering up after a spree. The next most common offenses were probably desertion and whatever might be covered by the phrase *neglect of duty*. One crew member was locked up for accidentally dropping a marlinspike from the rigging, another for slashing a man with a knife. Usually, prisoners were confined in irons for periods ranging from a few days up to two or three weeks. One of the longest sentences on record was that of Hugh McCormick, seaman, who spent fifty days in irons after attempting to desert. In some cases confinement in irons was a man's whole punishment; for others a flogging climaxed a week or two in confinement. The sternest punishments were those of repeaters, men who appeared to be confirmed troublemakers. On 16 December 1803 a Marine, George Crutch, was flogged twenty-four lashes for embezzling a pair of shoes and selling them. Seven weeks later Crutch was in trouble again. This time he had stolen a watch while on his post, thrown it overboard to escape detection, and then lied about the theft. His punishment was one of the severest Preble ever ordered—forty-eight lashes followed by four months in irons.

The basic legislation under which the U.S. Navy operated, "An Act for the Better Government of the Navy," passed in 1800, forbade any commanding officer on his own authority to flog a sailor more than twelve lashes; whippings in excess of that were supposed to be awarded by courts-martial. Despite the intent of the law, Preble, and most other captains, had a device for getting around the twelve-lash limit: since crime usually involved violation of several regulations, Preble would award twelve lashes for each offense. For instance, a sailor found guilty of drunkenness was also guilty of stealing his beverage from the ship's stores or of smuggling it into the *Constitution*; because of his inebriation, he would be unable to do his job and could be charged with neglect of duty, too. By assigning twelve lashes for each offense—drunkenness, theft or smuggling, neglect of duty—Preble could raise the punishment to thirty-six lashes. [. . .]

It is a risky business to compare Preble's discipline with that of his contemporaries. Some officers, Isaac Hull for one, made much less use of the lash than did Preble. By contrast, Preble was more lenient than John Rodgers, who, when he presided at courts-martial, sometimes awarded floggings through the fleet (in hundreds of lashes) and brandings. Preble might be rated as an extremely strict disciplinarian, but not a vindictive or brutal one. [. . .]

Three principles governed Preble's handling of disciplinary problems with officers. First, he had a low threshold of tolerance for courts-martial and courts of inquiry. He thought it a waste of time for valuable officers to sit listening to the sordid details of petty squabbles and uninteresting crimes when they should have been busy with more important duties. Invariably Preble sought to resolve disputes or handle disciplinary matters without convening courts. There were no courts-martial in the Mediterranean squadron during his command; only one matter had to be examined before a court of inquiry. Second, if Preble considered the offender a promising officer who had simply made a bad mistake, then counsel, a reprimand, or a minor administrative punishment—say, a couple of weeks under arrest with nothing for the offender to do but think about his misdeed—were the Commodore's preferred course of action. Third, should the offender appear to be incurable and undesirable as a naval officer, then Preble would try to maneuver him into resigning, using as a club the threat of a court-martial. [. . .]

Midshipman Thomas Baldwin was a source of distress to Preble from the day he joined the *Constitution* at Boston on 16 June 1803. His conduct was "in the highest degree ungentlemanly, being frequently intoxicated and *always* vulgar in his conversation and deportment." The *Constitution* had scarcely reached Gibraltar in September 1803 before Baldwin committed an act serious enough for Preble to get rid of him.

Baldwin went ashore at Gibraltar on liberty. After visiting one or more dram shops he ran into his shipmate, Midshipman Joseph Nicholson, and Midshipman John B. Nicholson, of the *John Adams*. Together they entered a store, and while John Nicholson was selecting a dirk, Thomas Baldwin shoplifted a sword knot. The trio had left the store and were walking down the street when the shopkeeper came running after them and accused John Nicholson of stealing the sword knot. Indignant, Nicholson denied the charge. A search was made. The stolen knot was found on Baldwin. Nicholson called Baldwin a "damned rascal," or, as Preble put it, "reproach[ed] him with the stigma his conduct had cast on the American officers," whereupon Baldwin drew his sword to attack Nicholson right there on the public street.

At last, Preble had Baldwin where he wanted him. As an alternative to court-martial, he drafted a letter of resignation from the Navy, had it neatly copied by one of his secretaries, and presented it to Baldwin. All Baldwin had to do was sign and hand over his warrant. In reporting the incident to Robert Smith, Preble said he hoped a court-martial could be dispensed with and Baldwin's resignation accepted, because "I studied the feelings of his family and friends, who are of the first respectability and I think entitled to consideration, especially when the service does not suffer too much by the indulgence." He did not add that, by forcing Baldwin to resign, he was choosing an infallible method of getting him out of the Navy. Convening a court-martial carried the risk of Baldwin being awarded a much milder punishment than dismissal from the Navy.

4 "COMMODORE JAMES BARRON: GUILTY AS CHARGED?"

Jay D. Smith

In the early U.S. Navy, a small officer corps sometimes descended into factionalism and favoritism. The parallel courts-martial of a commodore and the commander of his flagship reveal the degree to which officers thrived or failed because of their connections to other prominent officers—in an excellent example of early naval justice as politics by other means.

"COMMODORE JAMES BARRON: GUILTY AS CHARGED?"

By Jay D. Smith, U.S. Naval Institute *Proceedings* (November, 1967): 79–85.

Commodore James Barron was 39 when, in 1807, he received command of the U.S. Naval Forces in the Mediterranean and as his flagship the handy, Norfolk-built, 36-gun frigate *Chesapeake*.

Though he could draw deeply on the qualities of tenacity and the skill of his profession, James Barron was less resourceful in his liaisons with fellow officers. For one thing, he lacked that impulsive audacity that most of his contemporaries considered the only true valor and, unlike them, he professed no delight at all in the prospect of physical combat. He was by nature a reflective man, of inventive bent, and it seemed to many that he was not cut out for the Navy. He joined it certainly not from a burning ambition for glory, but perhaps because it was traditionally expected of a Barron; his father—for whom he was named—had been a prosperous shipmaster at 30 and Commander-in-Chief of the Virginia State Navy of the Revolution.

James Barron's reputation for pacifism had gathered momentum in the Mediterranean during the war with Tripoli; thus, he came aboard the frigate *Chesapeake* with his courage already suspect.

Two years earlier, in 1805, he had incurred the wrath of the redoubtable Captain John Rodgers. At that time, James was serving as captain of the *Essex* in the squadron commanded by his elder brother, Commodore Samuel Barron, who flew his broad pennant on the *President*. Samuel, however, lay confined to his sick bed, suffering from a strange, lingering fever; nevertheless, he continued to direct operations from Malta where the headquarters of the squadron was based. Rodgers, as next senior officer, was in command of the blockading force off Tripoli. Although more aggressive operations were planned for the summer, Rodgers was in a frenzy to press the attack against the city. He accused James of urging Samuel to retain command "while assuring me with the gravity of a Judas that he was prevailing upon him to resign."

Meanwhile, Colonel Tobias Lear, U.S. Consul General at Algiers, had been commissioned by President Thomas Jefferson to negotiate a treaty of peace. In a letter dated 18 May, Samuel Barron advised Lear that, in his opinion, the present was a moment highly favorable for opening peace negotiations. Lear had reached the same conclusion, and expressed his determination to meet the overtures lately made by the reigning Pasha.

Samuel then resigned his command in a letter to Rodgers on 22 May, and instructed him to assist Lear in formulating a treaty with Tripoli. Rodgers, now a commodore, issued a terse statement from his cabin in the *Constitution* that Samuel Barron's appeasement of the Barbary Powers "should forever damn his reputation." Since Samuel was ill and incapable of defending his reputation, James felt bound to notify Rodgers that in due time he would be called to account; whereupon Rodgers replied with a taunt of cowardice.

In addition, Samuel wrote Rodgers that in resigning his command, he nevertheless reserved the right to resume it in case his health was restored and the war lasted longer than he expected. Obviously, he hoped to recover soon and had no intention of leaving the station immediately. The peace treaty was duly signed on 3 June and not until 13 July did James speed home with his ailing brother.

When at last Rodgers followed the Barrons home it was he who flung the challenge at an apparently spiritless James, who now claimed that his own ill-health and the Department's orders would not permit a meeting. More than one officer found amusement in the spectacle of the pair reconnoitering each other, "unable to find a battleground." Friends at length arranged a bloodless settlement which, although it required Rodgers to withdraw his taunt of cowardice as an irritation of the moment, did nothing to lessen his repugnance toward the younger Barron.

Stephen Decatur had also become disenchanted with his old friend and mentor. He made it plain to both brothers that he considered James's part in the Rodgers affair highly reprehensible.

If Barron experienced any satisfaction from his new command in the *Chesapeake*, it must have been abruptly displaced by apprehension when he learned the identity of his officers.

Master-Commandant Charles Gordon was a foppish young man who strove for elegance in wit as he did in dress. He had served under Barron in the Mediterranean and the commodore considered him "an officer too much addicted to pleasure and parade to bend his mind to business." When Barron was informed of Gordon's assignment to the *Chesapeake*, he requested relief from command; Secretary of the Navy Robert Smith refused.

But Charles Gordon had no need of his commodore's approbation. His mother had been born a Nicholson of Maryland's Eastern Shore, and his uncles Samuel, James, and John, were all captains in the Continental Navy. Another uncle, Joseph Hopper Nicholson, was a former leader of the powerful House Ways and Means Committee. His cousin Hannah had married Albert Gallatin, Secretary of the Treasury, the man whose fine hand had rendered Robert

Smith's Navy Department nearly impotent, through his and the Jefferson administration's ideas for economizing.

As if the potential incompetence of his flag-captain was not enough to unsettle the commodore, the assignment of William Henry Allen as a ship's lieutenant must have seemed the nadir of his fortunes, for Allen was an intimate of John Rodgers, and he came aboard the *Chesapeake* already poisoned against his commanding officer "with all the prejudice his friend Rodgers could inculcate." The other officers were all to a greater or lesser degree bosom companions of Lieutenant Allen or admirers of Rodgers, and at least one of them had frequently reported to Rodgers on the state of Barron's "health" during their late feud.

Meanwhile, at Washington, a diplomatic flurry set the final backdrop for the bizarre incident which would confirm the whispered accusations of cowardice which swirled about the commodore. When the British complained that four deserters from His Majesty's frigate *Melampus* had been recruited for the *Chesapeake*, the commodore investigated and apparently satisfied both Secretaries Smith and James Madison and the British Consul John Hamilton that three of the men had indeed been signed on the American vessel but that they were in fact American citizens earlier pressed into British service; the fourth remained unaccounted for. But the case of a fifth man from the sloop *Halifax* was brought neither to the government's nor Barron's attention, the oversight no doubt that of John Hamilton, who failed to include in his note the name of the sailmaker. Now Jenkin Ratford, alias "John Wilson," a true if disloyal Englishman, labored on board the *Chesapeake* forgotten by all but a British squadron hovering off the Virginia Capes.

Charles Gordon brought the frigate down the Potomac to Hampton Roads where she would take on her commodore, the last of her crew, guns, and shot. In passing Mount Vernon, where every armed national vessel traditionally fired a salute to the memory of the late George Washington, Gordon found his sponges and cartridges were too large for the guns. This was attributed to the inefficiency of the Washington Navy Yard. Proceeding down river, the frigate's passage was studded with fatal accidents, desertions, and attempted mutiny.

When at last on 22 June, the *Chesapeake* pointed her bowsprit toward the Atlantic and got underway for the Mediterranean, her decks were a plateau of disorder, cluttered with baggage, canvas, cordage, empty water casks, and the armorer's forge and bellows. She carried 339 men and boys, several dependent passengers, and a Marine complement of 52.

The British squadron was clearly visible off Cape Henry Light. It had been there since the previous winter when it took up a blockade of two French vessels. When HMS *Leopard*, a 50-gun frigate, backed south and preceded the *Chesapeake* to sea, her maneuvers failed to arouse the commodore's suspicion. At half past three, the *Leopard* rounded up on the *Chesapeake*'s windward quarter and advanced to within 60 yards when her captain hailed; he bore dispatches for the American commodore, he said.

Minutes later, a British lieutenant named Meade climbed from a gig to the frigate's spar deck and was escorted below to the commodore's great cabin. The dispatch he brought bore the signature of Admiral George Cranfield Berkeley, Commander-in-Chief, the Royal Navy on the North American Station. It listed six British ships from which seamen had purportedly deserted to the *Chesapeake*, and required his captains to search the American vessel should they encounter her. Captain Salisbury Pryce Humphreys of the *Leopard* in his covering note conveyed his hopes that an adjustment could be reached without disturbing "the harmony subsisting between the two countries."

Commodore Barron explained to the lieutenant that the only deserters he was acquainted with were those from the *Melampus* and that that matter had been recently adjusted in Washington. Since the *Melampus* did not appear on the admiral's list, he could only presume that the British naval authorities, too, were satisfied with the results of his investigation. But what Barron did not know was that "John Wilson" of the *Halifax* (which ship *was* listed) lurked somewhere below decks, and that Captain Humphreys was very much aware of his presence.

After discussing the dispatch with a passenger and old friend, Doctor John Bullus, the commodore drafted a reply. "I am ... instructed," he closed, "never to permit the crew of any ship that I command, to be mustered by any other than their own officers; it is my disposition to preserve harmony; and I hope this answer to your dispatch will prove satisfactory." Barron had, in fact, received a specific reminder from Secretary Smith before sailing: America was a peaceful nation and "Our interests as well as good faith requires that we should cautiously avoid whatever may have a tendency to bring us into collision with any other power."

It was only after the lieutenant returned to his gig that Barron discovered the *Leopard* was cleared for action, gunports triced up, tompions removed, and Marines at station. He told Gordon to get the men to quarters quietly without benefit of the drum. Boys scurried below to the magazine for powder horns and matches; men were put to clearing the gun and spar decks. But it was too late.

Gazing toward the American frigate, Captain Humphreys called out something about being compelled to comply with orders. Commodore Barron, delaying for precious minutes, replied that he could not hear.

The first ball flew athwart the *Chesapeake*'s bow, soon followed by another. Then broadside after broadside was hurled into the frigate. Men were drenched in the blood of their companions as they cringed behind the silent guns. Only seven powder horns out of 54 on board were filled; the slow matches were not primed; even the loggerheads were cold. Commodore Barron could only stand by and watch his ship beaten into splinters while his own batteries stayed mute. Seven times wounded himself, he could not comprehend the inactivity of his officers. Captain Hall later testified that Barron, observing some of the rigging shot away, cried, "For God's sake, gentlemen. Will nobody do his duty? Look at those braces, and that rigging. Why are not stoppers put upon them?" In the confusion, Barron's latent distrust of his officers must have been confirmed by what he considered disloyalty and dereliction of duty.

Some minutes later, Barron requested Hall to ". . . go down to the gun deck and ask them for God's sake to fire one gun for the honour of the flag. I mean to strike." Using a hot coal from the galley, a lone gun was fired by Lieutenant Allen at the very moment when the commodore ordered the colors struck. The British boarded and took off not only "John Wilson" (found lurking in the coal hole), but the three *Melampus* men as well. Captain Humphreys deplored the necessity of the measures he had been forced to employ and refused Barron's invitation to accept the *Chesapeake* as a prize. Their governments were, after all, at peace.

The only alternative was to return to port. The commodore called a council of his officers to solicit their views of the afternoon's events.

At first no one spoke. Then Gordon broke the silence: although it was true that further bloodshed had been avoided by striking the colors, "a few broadsides would have been more to our credit." Lieutenant Montgomery Crane said, "It had been better if the *Chesapeake* were blown from under us than be thus dishonored." Lieutenant Allen went further. He could scarcely refrain from cursing the commodore. "We have disgraced ourselves," he said. Before any of the others could venture an opinion, Barron said he had heard enough and dismissed them.

The frigate crept back to port, her sails riddled and patched, colors missing, carrying three dead (one more would die) and 20 wounded.

The commodore's hastily written report of the encounter was borne to Secretary Smith by Captain Gordon "in order that you may have an opportunity of getting such information as you may wish." It breathed no trace of dissatisfaction with the conduct of his officers, though by now he was convinced of their dereliction. Perhaps he believed they would close ranks with him in the face of the official inquiry and public censure that was certain to engulf them all.

But the officers of the *Chesapeake* were less charitable than their commander. They were motivated by more personal considerations; prompt disavowal of Barron's surrender might relieve them of complicity. So, with the commodore's dispatch went another signed by the lieutenants and the sailing master demanding Barron's arrest on two charges: that on the probability of an engagement he had neglected to clear his ship for action; and that he had failed to do his utmost "to take or destroy a vessel which we conceive it his duty to have done." In reply to their petition, Secretary Smith complimented them on their action and promised it would be properly attended to.

Barron's prospects, never good, steadily worsened. While the nation clamored for war with England, he was relieved of command and the multiple wounds he had suffered kept him at home. He might have taken temporary comfort from the appointment of Commodore Edward Preble as President of the Court of Inquiry assembled to probe the encounter, but he was plunged into despair when Preble died in August and the post went to Commodore Alexander Murray, a cousin of Gordon, and an officer whom Barron once had privately criticized for his sloppy fitting out of the captured *Insurgente*. It had been at a time when confidences were brittle; word had eventually reached Murray, and Barron gained another foe.

The commodore's glimmering hope for an unbiased hearing vanished when Commodore John Rodgers was installed as President of the ensuing Court Martial. Young Stephen Decatur made manifest his own prejudice toward Barron when he was appointed to sit on the court. "It is probable that I am prejudiced against Commodore Barron," he wrote Secretary Smith. "Even prior to the attack my opinion of him as a soldier was not favorable." The Secretary denied his request for relief as he did several others, for there were already too few captains available to serve. Barron wanted to protest Decatur's inclusion but was dissuaded by his attorney. The Judge Advocate for both the Court of Inquiry and the Court Martial was Littleton Waller Tazewell, a staunch friend of the Nicholsons and also of Thomas Jefferson.

Barron, Gordon, Marine Captain John Hall, and Gunner William Hook were all to be tried separately for various offenses. It was made clear from the outset that Gordon was under no obligation to answer any questions put to him at the Barron trial if his replies would prejudice his own case that was to follow. He exercised this privilege frequently, so frequently in fact that Commodore Barron remarked in his defense plea, "A stronger motive operates upon him; the web of his destiny is interwoven with mine; my condemnation is the pledge of his acquittal; . . . To the prosecution his inmost soul is cheerfully unfolded; to me, he is cold as death; and silent as the tomb." Why? Because if Barron were to be acquitted of his charges, the guilt must fall on the shoulders of Charles Gordon.

From the wording of Admiral Berkeley's dispatch, the court determined that Barron should have expected an encounter; and his hastily worded report to the Secretary confirmed their opinion. Unfortunately, the only person who could have testified as to Barron's exact impressions upon receiving the dispatch was Dr. Bullus, who begged to be excused from the trial, and was not pressed to appear.

The commodore was finally acquitted of all but one charge: "For neglecting on the probability of an engagement to clear his ship for action." He was guilty of failing to sniff hostile intent and for this error in judgment was suspended from active service for five years, that is, until 8 February 1813.

The court next turned to Charles Gordon. He pleaded his own case without benefit of legal counsel. He did not deny that the general state of the vessel had been his responsibility. Placing himself at the mercy of his peers, he pointed out, however, that "If the guns were not securely fitted in their carriages, they certainly did not jump out that day. If the sponges and wads were not of the proper sizes, neither sponge nor wad was that day used. If the powder horns were not all filled, those which were filled were not used that day. If the matches were not primed, no effort was made to light them on that day. . . . if I have been guilty of omissions, therefore, this court will do me the justice to say that the disastrous results did not proceed from them. That they were mere neglects of duty, from which no evil consequence has been felt. . . . I feel confident that you will not say I have ever omitted anything which I ought to have done. . . ."

Barron's defense attempted to prove that he was misled on the state of the ship and introduced evidence in the form of a letter addressed to him by Captain Gordon before the ship sailed: "All station bills are completed. The guns are all charged and if possible we have an exercise this evening." Gordon refused to acknowledge that he had written the letter until it was repeatedly dangled under his nose. Nevertheless, the court remained prejudiced in favor of Gordon.

Charles Gordon had been derelict in his duty, and the court found him guilty as charged. Since "no evil" was said to have resulted from the neglects of which he stood accused, however, he was entitled to the most generous treatment. Never was the confidence of an accused in his judges more bountifully rewarded. He was sentenced to be privately reprimanded by the Secretary of the Navy, and it was added that since his offense had been "a very slight one," if a more lenient penalty had been available, the court would not have hesitated to impose it. Captain Hall of the Marines also received a verdict and sentence identical with those of Gordon. Gunner Hook was adjudged guilty of negligence in performing his duty and was dismissed from the service.

One does not need to dispute the judgment or the penalty in Barron's case in order to question whether Charles Gordon was so much less reprehensible that the court would, after finding him guilty of neglect of duty, seek the softest penalty it could find, and even announce that it had done so, as if in public apology for having heard his case at all.

How could the court so easily have condoned Gordon's neglect of a bounden duty to have his ship ready for instant engagement *at all times*, when it had just condemned Barron for failing to clear the same unprepared ship for action in the space of less than an hour?

The reason given is that "no evil" resulted from Gordon's omissions. But had the frigate been properly prepared for sea, 20 minutes would have sufficed to clear her decks and get her guns firing, according to Lieutenant Allen's testimony. And Barron had taken half an hour to answer Captain Humphreys' dispatch. The evil which certainly did result from Gordon's omissions was as much due to Gordon's neglect as to Barron's failure to detect promptly hostile intent.

The commodore went to his grave convinced that "There was an influence in the cabinet of that day which protected Captain Gordon." In view of Gordon's highly placed relatives, it would be difficult not to agree with Barron.

In later years, when the commodore was pressing for re-employment after his term of suspension, the *Chesapeake*'s Marine Captain John Hall unburdened his conscience by disclosing to Barron that the Judge Advocate had written both his own and Gordon's defenses. Indeed, stories were circulated around Norfolk that Charles Gordon himself had often been heard to boast of Tazewell's uncommon favor.

After the trial, Barron entered the merchant service and remained abroad until 1818, when he returned to the United States and again sought service in the Navy. The majority of naval officers opposed his readmission, most particularly Decatur, who was then on the Board of Naval Commissioners. Barron felt that his court-martial sentence had been "cruel and unmerited" and that the principal officers, by refusing him service, were adding injuries to what they had already done to him in the past. Always a jealous man, he brooded on his wrongs and became extremely touchy.

In reply to a real or fancied insult by Decatur, Barron commenced a correspondence that was exasperating and inflammatory on both sides. It eventually led him to challenge Decatur to a duel, which, according to the customs of the day, was the only way for men of honor to settle a dispute. Though in this case, Barron was considered the aggressor, Decatur's conduct was not above reproach.

On 22 March 1820, the duel took place at Bladensburg. Decatur was mortally wounded and died 12 hours later at his home. Barron was wounded in the thigh, but soon recovered. Shortly afterward, he was restored to active duty, but in spite of all his requests, he never commanded a ship or went to sea again. He served as commandant of the Norfolk and Philadelphia navy yards, and as governor of the naval asylum at Philadelphia, and died in 1851 at the venerable age of 83, the Navy's senior officer.

Yet, even today, public sentiment and the official record are in want of correction. *The Index for General Courts Martial and Courts of Inquiry*, 1799–1861, declares Barron's culpability as "Neglect of duty, and failing to encourage his men on board the Frigate Chesapeake—Confirmed: Thos. Jefferson."

5 "OLD MARINE CORPS: COURT MARTIAL OF A COMMANDANT"

LtCol Merrill Bartlett, USMC (Ret.)

Though it's a more ambiguous example, owing to the erratic behavior of the defendant, the court-martial of an early Marine Corps commandant presents another example of a politicized event in early naval justice.

"OLD MARINE CORPS: COURT MARTIAL OF A COMMANDANT"

By LtCol Merrill Bartlett, USMC (Ret.), U.S. Naval Institute *Proceedings* (June 1985): 69–72.

On 10 November, the Marine Corps' official birthday, a wreath is placed on the grave of each officer who had been a Commandant of the Marine Corps (CMC). But there is one exception. No one is sure where the fourth commandant, Anthony Gale, is buried.

Gale served only a brief period as Commandant—3 March 1819–16 October 1820. Yet his service to the Marine Corps and his country, and the political infighting surrounding his removal from office as a result of a court-martial, are illustrative of the often strange relationship that existed between the Marine

Corps and the Secretary of the Navy in the Corps' early years. And the machinations of some of Gale's fellow officers for the post of CMC probably contributed to his demise. [...]

When [Commandant Franklin] Wharton died, Gale was the senior officer in the Marine Corps, with an unfortunate reputation for a fondness for the bottle and a hot Irish temper; he did not appear to be much of a gentleman. Moreover, Gale had seen little combat by comparison with most of his contemporaries, and he often displayed a casual indifference to administrative procedures. With the possibility that Gale might become the next CMC, a flurry of political infighting for the Corps' highest post followed as some hoped that strict seniority—as had been the custom since 1798—would not observed. [Brevet Major Samuel] Miller hoped especially that he might receive the appointment. Several members of Congress and the Chief Clerk of the Department of the Navy wrote to President James Monroe extolling Miller's professional qualifications for the post. Miller even had the temerity to write directly to the President asking to be considered.

Gale, however, assumed correctly that he would receive the appointment on the basis of seniority, and on 3 March 1819 he became the Commandant of the Marine Corps. The Marine Corps that Gale inherited numbered 47 officers and 875 enlisted men, mostly providing detachments for 58 vessels of war of all sizes.

The duties of his office had changed little from those which the Department of the Navy had defined for the House of Representatives in 1803: recruiting, outfitting recruits, providing guards for naval vessels and yards, and disciplining and maintaining small arms for Marines ashore. In addition, the CMC administered the Marine Corps by corresponding with the Department of the Navy and handled all pay and accounts.

In contrast, the Navy of that era received most of its guidance directly from the Secretary of the Navy himself. Although the Board of Navy Commissioners had been in operation since January 1815, its duties remained mostly administrative in nature, leaving operational matters to the Office of the Secretary of the Navy. The small detachments of Marines in the Navy's ships helped maintain order and discipline among a mostly foreign-born enlisted force plagued by low pay, bad food, and dangerous work. Most Navy officers and government officials remained convinced that only the threat of the lash and a Marine guard kept this obstreperous rabble in check.

Whatever Gale's shortcomings as an administrator or Marine Corps professional, he understood all too clearly that the limits of his office needed to be defined. Many Marine Corps officers were in the habit of corresponding directly to the Secretary of the Navy or even to the President when they wanted a transfer or extended leave. The indefatigable [Major Archibald] Henderson even wrote to the Secretary of the Navy requesting permission to join General Andrew Jackson's expedition to Florida.

Gale charged into this administrative breach by taking his troubles directly to Smith Thompson, President James Monroe's Secretary of the Navy. A lawyer, Thompson was appointed to office on 1 January 1819 after the post was offered to Commodore John Rodgers, president of the Board of Commissioners, who declined it. Thompson did not leave a distinguishing stamp on the office, even absenting himself from his desk from 28 March to 20 December 1819. However, as unenthused as Thompson appeared to be with his political appointment, he did demand what he considered to be his prerogatives as secretary, and Gale came to be at loggerheads with him.

In August 1820, Gale wrote Thompson a long, rambling letter which outlined the problems of the CMC's command authority. In it, Gale asked that the limits of his office be defined. If the secretary responded at all, his answer has not survived. Gale had other problems at the time, unfortunately. After 30 August 1820, Brevet Major Miller signed all correspondence from Headquarters Marine Corps as Gale appeared to be on a drunken binge. Miller informed the Secretary of the Navy, and one of the strangest courts-martial in U.S. naval history followed.

In apparent compliance with the secretary's orders, Miller ordered a general court-martial for Gale on 7 September 1820, charging the CMC with:

- Habitual drunkenness in dram shops and in the streets of Washington, D.C.
- Conduct unbecoming an officer and gentleman, including visiting a house of ill-fame near the barracks, calling Lieutenant N. M. Desha, Paymaster of the Marine Corps, a "damned rascal, liar, and coward," and then threatening him, declaring in the streets near the barracks that he "did not care a damn for the President, Jesus Christ, or God Almighty"
- Signing a false statement (using a Marine Corps private as a waiter and coachman)
- Violating the orders of his arrest and leaving his quarters without permission

The membership of the court-martial contributed to the strange legal proceedings: an Army brigadier general, R. L. Jesup, served as president, alongside two field grade Army officers and two Marine Corps captains. Although preferring the charges, Miller prosecuted the case, and Desha, a witness for the prosecution, received orders as a supernumerary to the court-martial. Meanwhile, the secretary and Miller placed Gale under house arrest, which prevented him from gathering witnesses and evidence in his defense. At the trial, Gale pleaded that temporary derangement, not intoxication, precipitated his strange behavior and claimed a history of mental illness in his family. Unmoved, the court found Gale guilty.

On 19 October 1820, Miller informed Gale that the President had approved the findings of the court-martial, dismissing the CMC from the Marine Corps. As a postscript to the official letter ending Gale's career in naval service, Miller wished Gale would "correct a habit [drunkenness]."

Gale's wife appealed to the secretary after the trial. By then, the former CMC had been confined to a mental hospital, and his wife informed the secretary that Gale had first shown signs of mental instability in 1817. She wondered just how she and the children were to survive. Her letter to the secretary was poignant and moving: "... his head is silvered with age and service ... [he] never neglected his duty until it pleased heaven to visit him." [...]

Gale's demise and short commandancy provide a sorry interlude in the history of the Marine Corps' highest post. His untimely dismissal only underscored the political schemes afoot among many Marine Corps senior officers. While Gale's professional shortcomings were well known, he deserved better treatment at the hands of his fellow Marines. To a moralistic jurist like Secretary of the Navy Thompson, Gale must have been anathema. And Gale's randy behavior and bouts with the bottle, exacerbated perhaps by mental illness, made a change in the Commandancy of the Marine Corps easier to accomplish.

6 "ROBERT F. STOCKTON: NAVAL OFFICER AND REFORMER"

(Selection from chapter 5 of *Quarterdeck & Bridge*)

Harold D. Langley

The single chapter excerpted below covers considerable ground in the history of the early Navy. First, it shows the harm done to good military order by partiality and favoritism in naval justice. Second, it shows the efforts of an early Navy officer to swim against the tide, delivering well-reasoned discipline as a part of a larger effort within his command to establish a culture of professionalism. Finally, it describes the successful effort in 1850 to ban flogging as a naval punishment, and a failed effort soon after to restore it as a means of shipboard discipline.

"ROBERT F. STOCKTON: NAVAL OFFICER AND REFORMER"

By Harold D. Langley (Selection from chapter 5 of *Quarterdeck & Bridge: Two Centuries of American Naval Leaders*) edited by James C. Bradford (Naval Institute Press, 1997): 77–102.

[...] After the war with Algiers, Stockton returned to the Mediterranean in the new ship-of-the-line *Washington*, the flagship of Commodore Isaac Chauncey.

Peacetime routine was dull, and officers had few opportunities to advance themselves. Frustration often prompted younger officers to utter hostile, unguarded remarks that led to duels. Discipline among the officers deteriorated. Two events that took place in the squadron greatly influenced Stockton.

First, Captain John Orde Creighton of the *Washington* was brought to trial [*Editor's note:* in August 1816] for striking a midshipman, accusing him of lying, and threatening to throw him overboard. The court-martial board, with Commodore Oliver Hazard Perry presiding, did not allow the midshipman to present the testimony of two lieutenants and arbitrarily ended the trial. The court found Creighton not guilty. This verdict so outraged the midshipmen of the squadron that fifty-one of them sent a petition to Congress asking for protection from tyrannical officers. It was the view of members of Congress that the petition was insubordinate, and they took no action on it.

Another outrage took place when Commodore Perry, acting in an arbitrary manner, removed from command John Heath, the captain of the marines on *Java*. When the relief from command was not followed by charges, Heath sent a note to Perry and asked what the next step was to be. Perry summoned Heath to his cabin, and, during a high-pitched discussion, struck the marine. Heath proffered charges, with Perry making countercharges. The same court that had tried Creighton now tried Perry, and Creighton was one of the judges. The court found both men guilty but sentenced them only to a reprimand. Once again, the verdict outraged the junior officers. Fifty of them—midshipmen, lieutenants, and marines—sent a memorial to Congress that protested the partiality of the court-martial.

Stockton signed this memorial, which marked the real beginning of his interest in naval reform.

Although Stockton could do little to reform the Navy as a whole, he could do something about those under his immediate command. He set about teaching his subordinates his philosophy of command. Stockton believed that an officer must inspire his officers to respect him and to be deferential to his position and sense of honor. It was the commander's obligation to demonstrate to everyone his dedication to justice and fairness. An officer was expected to be a gentleman, and a gentleman should not do wrong himself or allow anyone else to do it without punishment. As for subordinates, they must respect and obey their superiors. One of the most basic lessons that all officers must learn, according to Stockton, was that they remain cool under all circumstances. "Remember, Gentlemen," he would say, "that there is always time enough to fight; keep cool; never get in a passion, under the grossest provocation."

The young lieutenant applied this principle in an effort to control dueling. Stockton himself was a good shot, and he fought duels with British officers in the Mediterranean in the interest of demanding respect for the officers of the U.S. Navy, not to avenge his personal honor. When an American midshipman challenged him to a duel, Stockton met the man ashore at the appointed place. The midshipman fired and missed. Stockton fired into the air. The seconds determined that honor had been satisfied. All involved in this encounter became firm friends of Stockton, and the midshipman became a zealous upholder of shipboard discipline.

Increasingly, Stockton devoted himself to compromising disputes between officers and discouraging duels. His success in this effort led others to enlist his efforts to arbitrate questions. In Stockton's view, it was rarely necessary for a gentleman to fight a duel. A gentleman was always willing to make whatever explanations were proper. If the offended person was also a gentleman, he would be satisfied with honest explanations. This code of conduct was palatable to junior officers because it came from someone who had proved his personal courage on a number of occasions.

Because he had some knowledge of the law and was a good speaker, Stockton found himself in demand as a counsel in courts-martial. In this, as in other affairs, he was a conscientious officer, and he had some successes in this area as well. It may well have pleased him to reflect that by a strange quirk of fate he was now acting as a lawyer, as his father and grandfather had done before him.

As a result of several disciplinary problems in the squadron, Commodore Charles Stewart relieved four officers and sent them to the sloop-of-war *Erie*, under Stockton's command, for passage home. Stockton made the journey during the winter and arrived in late January 1820 without any mishaps. Secretary of the Navy Smith Thompson expressed his satisfaction with Stockton's report of his voyage and added that it was "evidence of your active exertion, and prudence as commander of the ship." [. . .]

[. . .] [Stockton] was not interested in political office. He resigned his commission in the Navy on 28 May 1850 to devote himself to private affairs. In a letter to a Trenton newspaper in November 1850, Stockton turned down the suggestion that his name should be placed in nomination for the U.S. Senate. He hoped that the honor would go to someone who was pledged to uphold the Union. Members of the New Jersey state legislature believed that no one had a stronger dedication to the Union than Stockton. He was elected as a Democrat to the Thirty-second Congress, which met in special session on 4 March 1851.

During his time in the Senate he made speeches advocating improved harbor defenses and against intervention in European affairs, but his most famous effort came about as a result of an attempt to reintroduce punishment by flogging in the Navy.

Flogging in the Navy and merchant marine had been abolished by a provision in an appropriation bill passed on 28 September 1850. The President signed the bill into law, and Congress adjourned on the same day. Because no substitute punishments were indicated, there was a feeling in some parts of the Navy that the measure was hasty and ill conceived. The Secretary of the Navy received letters from officers who asked for instructions on how to deal with unruly seamen. The Secretary of the Navy asked Congress to revise the whole system of punishments at once. On 17 December 1851, Senator Richard Broadhead of Pennsylvania introduced a memorial, signed by a large number of citizens, urging that punishment by flogging be reintroduced. This stirred Stockton to action. After expressing his amazement that any group of people would advocate such a thing, Stockton gave notice that he would oppose the suggestion.

When the proposition was considered on 7 January 1852, Stockton was ready. He spoke with feeling about the superiority of the American sailor and how he had proved his worth in war and peace. Stockton protested: "The theory that the Navy cannot be governed, and that our national ships cannot be navigated, without the use of the lash, seems to me to be founded in that false idea that sailors *are not men*—not American citizens—have not the common feelings, sympathies, and honorable impulses of our Anglo-Saxon race." The commodore related how men would undergo all sorts of hardship for a commander they loved and who they believed cared for them. Punishment by flogging destroyed a sailor's self-respect, pride, and patriotism. A new and more civilized age had dawned. In the state prisons, the worst offenses were no longer punished by flogging. Why then, he asked, did people want to restore "this relic of barbarism" to the Navy?

Stockton went on to describe his own quarter century of association with seamen in various parts of the world. He told what they had done as infantry in the California campaigns. "American sailors, as a class," argued Stockton, "have loved their country as well, and have done more for her in peace and war, than any other equal number of citizens." Yet the sailor enjoyed little in the way of comfort, was treated as an outcast on shore, and often died poor. Some now argued that he should again be flogged like a felon. As far as he was concerned, said Stockton, he would rather see the Navy abolished than to see flogging restored. Officers of the Navy who thought that the sailor was more influenced by fear than by affection were wrong. "You can do infinitely more with him by rewarding him for his faithfulness than by flogging him for his delinquencies," Stockton asserted. It was much more effective to punish minor infractions by stopping the sailor's allowance of tobacco, tea, sugar, or coffee. To improve the Navy and its discipline, Stockton recommended a system of rewards and punishments, the abolition of the grog ration, and a restructuring of the recruiting service.

Efforts to refute Stockton's arguments were made by George E. Badger of North Carolina, a former Secretary of the Navy, and by Stephen Mallory of Florida, but they were futile. No one could bring to the subject the range of firsthand experience and conviction possessed by the commodore. The petition to reestablish flogging was referred to the Committee on Naval Affairs, where it died. The Congress now had to consider a new code of discipline. This code was not completed and enacted into law until 1862.

In beating back the effort to restore flogging, Stockton reached the apex of his career as a naval reformer. He was the right man in the right place to win the battle. No one could match his credentials. He had had a wide-ranging and full career and had proved himself successful in business, in politics, and as a naval officer. On board his own ship, he had demonstrated that a system of humane discipline was not only possible but also efficient. It was now up to other officers to learn how to apply those lessons. He had repaid his own men for their devotion. In the Senate of the United States, he had proclaimed the virtues of the American sailor. By his action in stopping the restoration of a cruel punishment, he helped to start a systematic reexamination of the whole body of regulations. The result was both a new code and a fresh perspective on how the Navy should function.

7 "THE *SOMERS*"

(Selection from chapters 7, 8, and 9 of *Mutiny*)

Leonard F. Guttridge

One of the most infamous courts-martial in Navy history wasn't actually a court-martial at all. In 1842 officers aboard a Navy brig-of-war concluded that a midshipman was conspiring with sailors to organize a mutiny, kill the captain, and seize the ship. They convened as an unofficial court, taking testimony from sailors and delivering guilty verdicts and death sentences they had no authority to impose. After the midshipman and two sailors were hanged at sea, a real court-martial tried the captain of the *Somers* for murder.

"THE *SOMERS*"

(Selection from chapters 7, 8, and 9 of *Mutiny: A History of Naval Insurrection*) by Leonard F. Guttridge (Naval Institute Press: 1992): 94–114.

In 1841 Mackenzie, aged thirty-eight, was promoted to commander and assigned to the steam frigate *Missouri*, from which vessel he sent Abel P. Upshur, the new secretary of the navy, his most detailed program yet on the subject of apprentices. It entailed the deployment of a vessel manned almost entirely by boys, who would thus receive their training at sea, the vessel functioning both as schoolship and cruiser. He thought a suitable ship would be

47

one of the navy's two new brigs, just completed at the New York and Boston navy yards. In his reply, dated 7 May 1842, Upshur replied that the department had been thinking along the same lines and had only awaited the availability of a suitable ship. That time had arrived. "The necessary orders will be immediately given to prepare the *Somers* for this purpose and you will be ordered to the command of her."

The *Somers* was a racily built brig-of-war, weighing little more than 250 tons and mounting ten 32-pound carronades on the spar deck. Like her sister, the *Bainbridge*, she was much oversparred—both vessels were fated to capsize and sink, with a heavy loss of life. The *Somers* measured 105 feet from prow to taffrail and 25 feet in the beam, her berth deck 17 feet wide and with only 58 inches of head room. To some of the 166 men and boys, more than half of them aged seventeen or under, who boarded the vessel at Brooklyn that midsummer, her living quarters must have appeared dismayingly cramped. Some may also have soon felt that the captain was a figure to be feared. Mackenzie was apprehensive that the boys included "too many children of foreigners . . . brought up precariously, dull-witted and far from robust." And the severity of his rule was manifest at the outset.

During the six weeks of final work before the *Somers* left on her maiden voyage Mackenzie inflicted about fifty separate punishments. Some were for desertion or theft, for which he ordered a dozen lashes, the maximum allowed, with the cat-o'-nine-tails. The busiest punitive instrument was the colt, a three-stranded rope frayed at the ends, and he ordered shirt-clad adolescents whipped 422 times for blaspheming, being unclean, fighting, losing a hammock, spitting, throwing tea or tobacco on the deck, and most frequently "skulking"— which usually meant attempting to shirk duty.

Writers who have dealt with the *Somers* tragedy concentrate mostly on Mackenzie's judgment and interpretation of events, some perceiving him as a victim of his own hyperimagination. They leave unanswered the question of how he rated as a disciplinarian, and few seem aware that even before he took command of the schoolship, Mackenzie had been described in public print as having a reputation for cruelty. [. . .]

[…] Officers began to notice signs that, it was afterward submitted, while not conceived as such at the time gave evidence of a mutinous conspiracy set in motion by Midshipman Philip Spencer. He mixed too little with his messmates and too freely with the crew and apprentices, some of whom he treated to liquor and tobacco and whose palms he read. He was given to enigmatic smiles and "a strange flashing of the eyes"; he cursed the captain behind his back, babbled of piracy, and searched maps for the Isle of Pines, a buccaneer's hangout west of Cuba. Michael H. Garty, six months a marine and a sergeant by virtue of his post on the *Somers* as master-at-arms, would remember Spencer's rambling on about seizing the ship and throwing the officers over the side. The midshipman had also displayed considerable interest in how many of the muskets in Garty's charge were kept loaded. Why had Garty not thought any of Spencer's talk worth reporting to the captain? "Because I had no suspicion of him."

Midshipman Rodgers would tell of Spencer's "mutinous expressions" while unable to recall his actual words. Purser's Mate Wales remembered the words— Spencer said he would love to throw the captain overboard and, by God, would do it yet—but "did not know at the time that these were mutinous expressions." To another midshipman Spencer said it would be easy to murder the captain and seize the vessel, and he sketched a pirate ship complete with skull and crossbones. He got Boatswain's Mate Cromwell to state the best means of disguising the brig—"by shipping the bowsprit aft"—and in a reference that begs further amplification, Captain Mackenzie would recall someone's telling him that Spencer had amused the crew by making music with his jaw: he had the knack of "throwing his jaw out of joint, and by the contact of the bones playing with accuracy and elegance a variety of airs." Sinister or merely bizarre, these characteristics were allegedly observed over a span of some eight weeks. Yet the captain was unaware of trouble and "could not forbear treating with ridicule" the extraordinary report, made in his cabin by Lieutenant Gansevoort on Saturday morning, 26 November, that "a conspiracy existed on board the brig, to capture her, murder the commander, the officers, and most of the crew, and convert her into a pirate, and that Acting Midshipman Philip Spencer was at the head of it." […]

Meanwhile, the seven officers whose advice [Mackenzie] awaited were assembled around a small table in the wardroom and had apparently decided to act less as an advisory board than as a grand jury. Lieutenant Gansevoort was to say that Mackenzie's letter ordered them to investigate the guilt of Spencer, Cromwell, and Small. According to the ship's log, Mackenzie's injunction was not only to probe their guilt but, if guilt was established, suggest "the best mode of disposing of them under the existing circumstances." If this latter request is true, much of the significance was conveyed verbally, for the letter itself contains no such specifics.

Thirteen witnesses were heard one by one. Not that "witnesses" is the correct word, except perhaps as applied to Purser's Steward Wales. In response to leading questions, their statements—taken under oath; noted in pencil by Purser Heiskell and Oliver Perry, the captain's clerk; finally read over to each; and signed or marked—consisted mostly of scattered thoughts and vague recollections, scarcely the substance even of gossip. Spencer and Cromwell had often been seen in furtive talk. The ship was not safe while they and Small remained alive. Some of the black galley cooks were in league with them. Some of the apprentices too. Cromwell was a desperate character; the damned son-of-a-bitch should hang. "Mr. Spencer told me if he knew where the keys lay, he would first take the arms and then secure the captain and officers. . . ." This was from the ailing Sergeant Garty, evidently asked by no one why he had not alerted the captain. The fullest "statement" was that of James Wales, its purport the conversation on the booms. Spencer had begun by asking Wales if he feared death and could kill a man. Wales gave him a meandering reply. Spencer then described his planned mutiny. After killing the captain, "Mr. Spencer was to go down in the wardroom and there, with his own hands, murder the wardroom officers, while they were asleep." The brig would be taken to the Isle of Pines or another pirate haunt. [. . .]

The council in the wardroom carried over into the following morning, 1 December. Not every officer stayed throughout, some came and went. At no time were any of the prisoners brought before it. They did not even know that they were being tried. There is a story, impossible to confirm, that Lieutenant Gansevoort twice emerged to tell his captain that they had insufficient evidence of the prisoners' guilt and that each time Mackenzie sent him back to secure a conviction. With or without such pressure from the captain, the result was a unanimous conclusion, delivered to Mackenzie as a letter consisting almost entirely of a 212-word sentence. Spencer, Cromwell, and Small were guilty of an intent to commit mutiny. Since the extent of their conspiracy was unknown and contingencies were impossible to foresee, it was unsafe to carry them home, and for the sake of the ship and the lives of the rest "they should be put to death, in a manner best calculated as an example to make a beneficial impression upon the disaffected." [. . .]

In those final moments Cromwell was heard to protest his innocence and to express concern for his wife, Small to lament for "my poor old mother." Lieutenant Gansevoort thought that he heard Spencer ask the captain to consider whether he might be acting too hastily. Gansevoort's testimony, with that of Mackenzie and Purser's Steward Wales, would tell of final handshakes, some flow of tears, and pleas from contrite transgressors for forgiveness. The three were escorted forward and helped upon hammock netting stacked port and starboard near each gangway. A black neckerchief found in Spencer's locker was placed over his face, and a frock or jumper hooded each of the others. In the log's terse words, "bent the starboard outer whip onto Acting Midshipman Spencer, the inner one onto Seaman Elisha Small, and the larboard one onto Boatswain's Mate Samuel Cromwell." When the ropes were thus fastened about their throats, Mackenzie mounted the trunk house, from which dais he ordered the executions carried out. The log suffices: "At 2.15 fired a weather gun and ran the prisoners up to the yardarm." [. . .]

When the court of inquiry exonerated Mackenzie, holding his "immediate execution of the ringleaders demanded by duty and justified by necessity," cynics apprehended a whitewash. Simon Cameron, a future successor to John Spencer in the War Department, called the hanging of his son "cowardly butchery" and anticipated Mackenzie's upcoming court-martial as another "mockery of justice." Mackenzie requested that procedure himself to head off his arrest and trial for murder in a civil court, something the family of Boatswain's Mate Samuel Cromwell, covertly goaded by Secretary Spencer or his friends, had taken steps to bring about.

"Careworn and anxious," Mackenzie stood again in the great cabin of the *North Carolina*, charged with murder, illegal punishment, oppression, cruelty, and conduct unbecoming an officer, to all of which he pleaded not guilty. Heard by a panel of fourteen officers, most of the testimony echoed that of the court of inquiry. Sergeant Garty of the marines reiterated his belief that mutiny was planned and that an attempted rescue of Mackenzie's prisoners was likely to have succeeded. Discussion turned on whether they could have been carried into St. Thomas and transferred to another American vessel of war. Mackenzie's pen was again at work, on a hurried document for the court. St. Thomas was distant by some ten days' sailing when he had to contend with "the daily and hourly increasing insubordination of the crew." Besides, he could not be sure that the *Vandalia* or some other American man-of-war would be in harbor. It went without saying that from no other source would he have sought help. "A naval commander can never be justified in invoking foreign aid in reducing an insubordinate crew to obedience."

The trial had lasted about two months when Mackenzie's counsel read his defense. Even the evidence of "seemingly trifle incidents . . . looks and motions . . . significant enough to those who see them" bore onto the existence of a mutinous conspiracy: "Such is the character of mutiny." And in this instance, mutiny beyond the reach of statute law and with ever-growing prospects of success. "Never was a crew where malcontents could have had a fairer chance of making proselytes." Alone on the ocean, unable to invoke a regular court-martial, what was the commander to do? Given all circumstances, he had only one choice. "Necessity stood stern umpire." The judge advocate agreed, his closing remarks offering yet another definition of mutiny: "The intent or act to supersede lawful authority, or resist it, or bring it into contempt." Mackenzie was acquitted of all charges.

Three days after the verdict was announced, Surgeon Leacock of the *Somers*, who despite his failing health had joined his fellow officers in public support of their accused captain, was found dead of a self-inflicted wound in the brig's gun room. Mackenzie was not remotely the type to have sought release from woe in suicide, but his spirits were sorely tested in the months and years that followed. Hardly had the trial ended when Secretary Upshur removed him from command of the *Somers*, an action that Mackenzie, considering the legal vindication he had won, found "mortifying." And when an obviously impatient Upshur inquired of him about the twelve prisoners for whose expected trial the court remained in session, a weary Mackenzie replied that he no longer wished to prefer charges against them. They were released and the court adjourned.

8 "UTTERLY REPUGNANT TO THE SPIRIT OF OUR DEMOCRATIC INSTITUTIONS"

(Selection from chapters 26, 27, 35, 36, 86, and 87 of *White-Jacket or The World in a Man-of-War*)

Herman Melville

Moby Dick author **Herman Melville** served on a Navy frigate, the *United States*, in 1843. His fictionalized account of life on a man-of-war vividly illustrates three themes about naval justice. I have divided these three themes under my own headings: "Mad Jack" tells about an instance in which the captain of a warship destroyed his own authority, making it impossible for him to bring a subordinate to justice for an act of willful disobedience. "Punishment of Common Sailors" is Melville's attack on flogging as an unmanly and unrepublican practice, unsuited for the punishment of Americans. And "Ushant's Beard" describes a question that the U.S. armed forces never fully resolve: Where does military control of armed forces personnel end, and the autonomy of a person serving in uniform begin? Ushant's punishment can be compared to the 1803 and 1805 courts-martial of Col. Thomas Butler, USA, over his refusal to obey orders to cut his hair.

"UTTERLY REPUGNANT TO THE SPIRIT OF OUR DEMOCRATIC INSTITUTIONS"

(Selection from chapters 26, 27, 35, 36, 86, and 87 of *White-Jacket or The World in a Man-of-War*) by Herman Melville (Naval Institute Press, 1988): 127–34; 171–77; 411–16.

Mad Jack

About midnight, when the starboard watch, to which I belonged, was below, the boatswain's whistle was heard, followed by the shrill cry for "*All hands take in sail!* jump, men and save ship!"

Springing from our hammocks, we found the frigate leaning over to it so steeply, that it was with difficulty we could climb the ladders leading to the upper deck.

Here the scene was awful. The vessel seemed to be sailing on her side. The main-deck guns had several days previous been run in and housed, and the port-holes closed, but the lee carronades on the quarter-deck and forecastle were plunging through the sea, which undulated over them in milk-white billows of foam. With every lurch to leeward the yard-arm ends seemed to dip in the sea, while forward the spray dashed over the bows in cataracts, and drenched the men who were on the fore-yard. By this time the deck was alive with the whole strength of the ship's company, five hundred men, officers and all, mostly clinging to the weather bulwarks. The occasional phosphorescence of the yeasting sea cast a glare upon their uplifted faces, as a night fire in a populous city lights up the panic-stricken crowd.

In a sudden gale, or when a large quantity of sail is suddenly to be furled, it is the custom for the First Lieutenant to take the trumpet from whoever happens then to be officer of the deck. But Mad Jack had the trumpet that watch; nor did the First Lieutenant now seek to wrest it from his hands. Every eye was upon him, as if we had chosen him from among us all, to decide this battle with the elements, by single combat with the spirit of the Cape; for Mad Jack was the saving genius of the ship, and so proved himself that night. I owe this right hand, that is this moment flying over my sheet, and all my present being to Mad

Jack. The ship's bows were now butting, battering, ramming, and thundering over and upon the head seas, and with a horrible wallowing sound our whole hull was rolling in the trough of the foam. The gale came athwart the deck, and every sail seemed bursting with its wild breath.

All the quarter-masters, and several of the forecastle-men, were swarming round the double-wheel on the quarter-deck. Some jumping up and down, with their hands upon the spokes; for the whole helm and galvanized keel were fiercely feverish, with the life imparted to them by the tempest.

"Hard *up* the helm!" shouted Captain Claret, bursting from his cabin like a ghost in his night-dress.

"Damn you!" raged Mad Jack to the quarter-masters; "hard *down*—hard *down*, I say, and be damned to you!"

Contrary orders! But Mad Jack's were obeyed. His object was to throw the ship into the wind, so as the better to admit of close-reefing the top-sails.

[. . .]

In time of peril, like the needle to the load-stone, obedience, irrespective of rank, generally flies to him who is best fitted to command. The truth of this seemed evinced in the case of Mad Jack, during the gale, and especially at that perilous moment when he countermanded the Captain's order at the helm. But every seaman knew, at the time, that the Captain's order was an unwise one in the extreme; perhaps worse than unwise.

These two orders, given by the Captain and his Lieutenant, exactly contrasted their characters. By putting the helm *hard up*, the Captain was for *scudding*; that is, for flying away from the gale. Whereas, Mad Jack was for running the ship into its teeth. It is needless to say that, in almost all cases of similar hard squalls and gales, the latter step, though attended with more appalling appearances, is, in reality, the safer of the two, and the most generally adopted.

Scudding makes you a slave to the blast, which drives you headlong before it; but *running up into the wind's eye* enables you, in a degree, to hold it at bay. Scudding exposes to the gale your stern, the weakest part of your hull; the contrary course presents it to your bows, your strongest part. As with ships, so with men; he who turns his back to his foe gives him an advantage. Whereas, our ribbed chests, like the ribbed bows of a frigate, are as bulkheads to dam off an onset.

That night, off the pitch of the Cape, Captain Claret was hurried forth from his disguises, and, at a manhood-testing conjuncture, appeared in his true colors. A thing which every man in the ship had long suspected that night was proved true. Hitherto, in going about the ship, and casting his glances among the men, the peculiarly lustreless repose of the Captain's eye—his slow, even, unnecessarily methodical step, and the forced firmness of his whole demeanor—though, to a casual observer, seemingly expressive of the consciousness of command and a desire to strike subjection among the crew—all this, to some minds, had only been deemed indications of the fact that Captain Claret, while carefully shunning positive excesses, continually kept himself in an uncertain equilibrio between soberness and its reverse; which equilibrio might be destroyed by the first sharp vicissitude of events.

And though this is only a surmise, nevertheless, as having some knowledge of brandy and mankind, White-Jacket will venture to state that, had Captain Claret been an out-and-out temperance man, he would never have given that most imprudent order to *hard up* the helm. He would either have held his peace, and stayed in his cabin, like his gracious majesty the Commodore, or else have anticipated Mad Jack's order, and thundered forth "Hard down the helm!"

To show how little real sway at times have the severest restrictive laws, and how spontaneous is the instinct of discretion in some minds, it must here be added, that though Mad Jack, under a hot impulse, had countermanded an order of his superior officer before his very face, yet that severe Article of War, to which he thus rendered himself obnoxious, was never enforced against him. [. . .]

Punishment of Common Sailors

[. . .] In the American Navy there is an everlasting suspension of the Habeas Corpus. Upon the bare allegation of misconduct, there is no law to restrain the Captain from imprisoning a seaman, and keeping him confined at his pleasure. While I was in the Neversink, the Captain of an American sloop of war, from undoubted motives of personal pique, kept a seaman confined in the brig for upward of a month.

Certainly the necessities of navies warrant a code for its government more stringent than the law that governs the land; but that code should conform to the spirit of the political institutions of the country that ordains it. It should not convert into slaves some of the citizens of a nation of freemen. Such objections can not be urged against the laws of the Russian Navy (not essentially different from our own), because the laws of that Navy, creating the absolute one-man power in the Captain, and vesting in him the authority to scourge, conform in spirit to the territorial laws of Russia, which is ruled by an autocrat, and whose courts inflict the *knout* upon the subjects of the land. But with us it is different. Our institutions claim to be based upon broad principles of political liberty and equality. Whereas, it would hardly affect one iota the condition on shipboard of an American man-of-war's man, were he transferred to the Russian Navy and made a subject of the Czar.

As a sailor, he shares none of our civil immunities; the law of our soil in no respect accompanies the national floating timbers grown thereon, and to which he clings as his home. For him our Revolution was in vain; to him our Declaration of Independence is a lie.

[...]

Or will you say that a navy officer is a man, but that an American-born citizen, whose grandsire may have ennobled him by pouring out his blood at Bunker Hill—will you say that, by entering the service of his country as a common seaman, and standing ready to fight her foes, he thereby loses his manhood at the very time he most asserts it? Will you say that, by so doing, he degrades himself to the liability of the scourge, but if he tarries ashore in time of danger, he is safe from that indignity? All our linked states, all four continents of mankind, unite in denouncing such a thought.

We plant the question, then, on the topmost argument of all. Irrespective of incidental considerations, we assert that flogging in the Navy is opposed to the essential dignity of man, which no legislator has a right to violate; that it is oppressive, and glaringly unequal in its operations; that it is utterly repugnant to the spirit of our democratic institutions; indeed, that it involves a lingering trait of the worst times of a barbarous feudal aristocracy; in a word, we denounce it as religiously, morally, and immutably *wrong*.

No matter, then, what may be the consequences of its abolition; no matter if we have to dismantle our fleets, and our unprotected commerce should fall a prey to the spoiler, the awful admonitions of justice and humanity demand that abolition without procrastination; in a voice that it not to be mistaken, demand that abolition to-day. It is not a dollar-and-cent question of expediency; it is a matter of *right and wrong*. And if any man can lay his hand on his heart, and solemnly say that this scourging is right, let that man but once feel the lash on his own back, and in his agony you will hear the apostate call the seven heavens to witness that it is *wrong*. And, in the name of immortal manhood, would to God that every man who upholds this thing were scourged at the gangway till he recanted.

[...]

[...] The amount of flogging on board an American man-of-war is, in many cases, in exact proportion to the professional and intellectual incapacity of her officers to command. Thus, in these cases, the law that authorizes flogging does but put a scourge into the hand of a fool. [...]

Ushant's Beard

Though many heads of hair were shorn, and many fine beard reaped that day, yet several still held out, and vowed to defend their sacred hair to the last gasp of their breath. These were chiefly old sailors—some of them petty officers—who, presuming upon their age or rank, doubtless thought that, after so many had complied with the Captain's commands, *they*, being but a handful, would be exempted from compliance, and remain a monument to our master's clemency.

That same evening, when the drum beat to quarters, the sailors went sullenly to their guns, and the old tars who still sported their beards stood up, grim, defying, and motionless, as the rows of sculptured Assyrian kings, who, with their magnificent beards, have recently been exhumed by Layard.

When the proper time arrived, their names were taken down by the officers of divisions, and they were afterward summoned in a body to the mast, where the Captain stood ready to receive them. The whole ship's company crowded to the spot, and, amid the breathless multitude, the venerable rebels advanced and unhatted.

It was an imposing display. They were old and venerable mariners; their cheeks had been burned brown in all latitudes, wherever the sun sends a tropical ray. Reverend old tars, one and all; some of them might have been grandsires, with grandchildren in every port around the world. They ought to have commanded the veneration of the most frivolous or magisterial beholder. Even Captain Claret they ought to have humiliated into deference. But a Scythian is touched with no reverential promptings; and, as the Roman student well knows, the august Senators themselves, seated in the Senate-house, on the majestic hill of the Capitol, had their holy beards tweaked by the insolent chief of the Goths.

Such an array of beards! spade-shaped, hammer-shaped, dagger-shaped, triangular, square, peaked, round, hemispherical, and forked. But chief among them all, was old Ushant's, the ancient Captain of the Forecastle. Of a Gothic venerableness, it fell upon his breast like a continual iron-gray storm.

Ah! old Ushant, Nestor of the Crew! It promoted my longevity to behold you.

[...]

The rebel beards, headed by old Ushant's, streaming like a Commodore's *bougee*, now stood in silence at the mast.

"You knew the order!" said the Captain, eying them severely; "what does that hair on your chins?"

"Sir," said the Captain of the Forecastle, "did old Ushant ever refuse doing his duty? did he ever yet miss muster? But, sir, old Ushant's beard is his own!"

"What's that, sir? Master-at-arms, put that man into the brig."

"Sir," said the old man, respectfully, "the three years for which I shipped are expired; and though I am perhaps bound to work the ship home, yet, as matters are, I think my beard might be allowed me. It is but a few days, Captain Claret."

"Put him into the brig!" cried the Captain; "and now, you old rascals!" he added, turning round upon the rest, "I give you fifteen minutes to have those beards taken off; if they then remain on your chins, I'll flog you—every mother's son of you!—though you were all my own godfathers!"

The band of beards went forward, summoned their barbers, and their glorious pennants were no more. In obedience to orders, they then paraded themselves at the mast, and, addressing the Captain, said, "Sir, our *muzzle-lashings* are cast off!"

Nor is it unworthy of being chronicled, that not a single sailor who complied with the general order but refused to sport the vile *regulation-whiskers* prescribed by the Navy Department. No! like heroes they cried, "Shave me clean! I will not wear a hair, since I can not wear all!"

On the morrow, after breakfast, Ushant was taken out of irons, and, with the master-at-arms on one side and an armed sentry on the other, was escorted along the gun-deck and up the ladder to the main-mast. There the Captain stood, firm as before. They must have guarded the old man thus to prevent his escape to the shore, something less than a thousand miles distant at the time.

"Well, sir, will you have that beard taken off? you have slept over it a whole night now; what do you say? I don't want to flog an old man like you, Ushant!"

"My beard is my own, sir!" said the old man, lowly.

"Will you take it off?"

"It is mine, sir!" said the old man, tremulously.

"Rig the gratings!" roared the Captain. "Master-at-arms, strip him! quartermasters, seize him up! boatswain's mates, do your duty!"

While these executioners were employed, the Captain's excitement had a little time to abate; and when, at last, old Ushant was tied up by the arms and legs, and his venerable back was exposed—that back which had bowed at the guns of the frigate *Constitution* when she captured the *Guérrière*—the Captain seemed to relent.

"You are a very old man," he said, "and I am sorry to flog you; but my orders must be obeyed. I will give you one more chance; will you have that beard taken off?"

"Captain Claret," said the old man, turning round painfully in his bonds, "you may flog me, if you will; but, sir, in this one thing I can *not* obey you."

"Lay on! I'll see his backbone!" roared the Captain in a sudden fury.

"By heaven!" thrillingly whispered Jack Chase, who stood by, "it's only a halter; I'll strike him!"

"Better not," said a top-mate; "it's death, or worse punishment, remember."

"There goes the lash!" cried Jack. "Look at the old man! By G–d, I can't stand it! Let me go, men!" and with moist eyes Jack forced his way to one side.

"You, boatswain's mate," cried the Captain, "you are favoring that man! Lay on soundly, sir, or I'll have your own *cat* laid soundly on you."

One, two, three, four, five, six, seven, eight, nine, ten, eleven, twelve lashes were laid on the back of that heroic old man. He only bowed over his head, and stood as the Dying Gladiator lies.

"Cut him down," said the Captain.

"And now go and cut your own throat," hoarsely whispered an old sheet-anchor-man, a mess-mate of Ushant's.

When the master-at-arms advanced with the prisoner's shirt, Ushant waived him off with the dignified air of a Brahim, saying, "Do you think, master-at-arms, that I am hurt? I will put on my own garment. I am never the worse for it, man; and 'tis no dishonor when he who would dishonor you, only dishonors himself."

"What says he?" cried the Captain; "what says that tarry old philosopher with the smoking back? Tell it to me, sir, if you dare! Sentry, take that man back to the brig! Stop! John Ushant, you have been Captain of the Forecastle; I break you. And now you go into the brig, there to remain till you consent to have that beard taken off."

"My beard is my own," said the old man, quietly. "Sentry, I am ready."

And back he went into durance between the guns; but after lying some four or five days in irons, an order came to remove them; but he was still kept confined.

Books were allowed him, and he spent much time in reading. But he also spent many hours in braiding his beard, and interweaving it with strips of red bunting, as if he desired to dress out and adorn the thing which had triumphed over all opposition.

He remained a prisoner till we arrived in America; but the very moment he heard the chain rattle out of the hawse-hole, and the ship swing to her anchor, he started to his feet, dashed the sentry aside, and gaining the deck, exclaimed, "At home, with my beard!"

His term of service having some months previous expired, and the ship being now in harbour, he was beyond the reach of naval law, and the officers durst not molest him. But without unduly availing himself of these circumstances, the old man merely got his bag and hammock together, hired a boat, and throwing himself into the stern, was rowed ashore, amid the unsuppressible cheers of all hands. It was a glorious conquest over the Conqueror himself, as well worthy to be celebrated as the Battle of the Nile.

9 "HE SERVED ON SAMAR"

Capt Paul Melshen, USMCR

Examining courts-martial over war crime allegations, an article written by a post–Vietnam War Marine Corps officer describes a controversy over the extrajudicial execution of Filipinos by an officer in a much earlier war. It presents questions that will always arise in time of war. This article can be read alongside the later essay by Gary Solis, near the end of this anthology, on courts-martial over the wartime killing of Iraqi detainees by American soldiers and Marines.

"HE SERVED ON SAMAR"

By Capt Paul Melshen, USMCR, U.S. Naval Institute *Proceedings* (November 1979): 43–48.

During the early afternoon of 20 January 1902, First Lieutenant John H. A. Day, U.S. Marine Corps, marched nine Filipinos, natives of the island of Samar, under guard of a detachment of U.S. Marines down the main street of Basey, Samar. Upon reaching the town plaza, Day ordered his detachment of marines to execute the Filipinos by firing squad. The execution of one Filipino had already been carried out earlier that day, and one more was yet to follow. Day had been following orders of his immediate senior officer, Major and Brevet Lieutenant Colonel Littleton Waller Tazewell Waller. On 17 March 1902, Major Waller was arraigned in Manila and tried on a charge of murder by a U.S. Army court-martial. Waller's court-martial was to become an ambiguous segment of Marine Corps history.

Marine Corps ground involvement in the Philippines began on 3 May 1898, two days after Commodore George Dewey's victory over the Spanish at Manila Bay, when First Lieutenant Dion Williams and a detachment of Marines from the USS *Baltimore* planted an American flag at the Spanish naval station in Cavite. The Treaty of Paris, signed on 10 December 1898, ended America's war with Spain, but not its military involvement in the Philippines. For the next six years, U.S. armed forces fought against Filipino insurrectionists. From 1898 until the fall of 1901, marines took part in a number of operations against the insurrectionists, primarily on the island of Luzon, making several amphibious landings.

By the fall of 1901, U.S. military actions against insurrectionists on Luzon had come to an end. General Emilio Aguinaldo, leader of that island's insur-rectionists, had surrendered to the American forces on 1 April 1901 and swore allegiance to the United States. Later that same month, he issued a manifesto to his Filipino followers to "lay down their arms for 'the complete termination of hostilities.'" The government of Luzon was now in the hands of American civilian authorities. In two provinces, Batangas and the island of Samar, there were still hostilities. On Samar the insurrectionists were led by the Filipino General Vincente Lucban. American supervision of these provinces was under the direction of Army Major General Adna Chaffee, who had taken over com-mand from General Arthur MacArthur in July 1901.

Located in the equatorial tropics, Samar was completely engulfed with dense jungles. Not only did American forces have to endure heat, humidity, incessant rain, and dense vegetation, but in addition, they had to contend with snakes, leeches, and malaria-infested mosquitoes. Smallpox was also running rampant on the island. The hellish conditions on Samar in some instances drove men insane.

Lucban used the climate and the terrain of Samar to his advantage in his guerrilla war against the Americans. He had been on Samar for more than a year before the first American troops arrived. This had allowed him to recruit among the natives intensively, and by the time the American troops did arrive, most of the natives were either in Lucban's command or in sympathy with the insurrectionists. Lucban's control over the natives was pure tyranny. He would shoot anyone who failed to support him, including Spanish priests. He once wrapped the head of a pro-American Filipino in a kerosene-drenched American flag and set a torch to it while the man was still alive.

Most American commanders, Waller included, based their operations on the fact that the majority of the natives of Samar were hostile to U.S. actions and could not be trusted, despite pretenses by the villagers to be pro-American, and that many of these supposedly pro-American villagers were, in fact, members of Lucban's command. Because of this support by the populace for the insurrectionists, along with the hellish conditions of the natural environment, the U.S. Army was able to secure only a few coastal towns on Samar, enabling Lucban to control the hinterland.

Company C, 9th Infantry, arrived at Balangiga, Samar, on 11 August 1901, commanded by Captain Thomas W. Connell, U.S. Army. Connell, a strong advocate of President William McKinley's "benevolent assimilation," attempted to establish this policy at Balangiga. Connell's naive assumption that since "benevolent assimilation" seemed to be working on Luzon, it could also work on Samar, proved catastrophic. Samar was populated by an extremely violent, primitive society. Because of cultural differences and the inhabitants' hostility toward the American presence on the island, assimilation was impossible. One officer of the 9th Infantry testified later that he considered the natives ". . . savages; they were low in intelligence, treacherous, cruel; seemed to have no feeling for their families or anyone else."

On 28 September, led by town officials and members of the population of Balangiga, Lucban's forces plotted a surprise attack on Company C. Only 26 of the 74 American soldiers survived the massacre. Most were tortured to death and their bodies mutilated:

". . . A smoldering fire [was] still burning about the face of Captain Connell. A deep wound across the face of Lieutenant Bumpus had been filled with jam, and one of the enlisted men 'had his abdomen cut open and codfish and flour put in the wound.'"

Connell's assessment of the situation on Samar had proven fatal.

The insurrectionists on Samar habitually committed atrocities, such as body mutilation of dead soldiers, during their guerrilla warfare against the Americans. Lucban refused to honor any rules of warfare:

". . . The dead were mutilated. . . . No prisoners were taken. Noncombatants were put to death. Poison was used. Flags of truce were not respected. The personnel of the insurrectionary forces was composed, in numerous instances of males under military age, who were old enough to assist in military operations, but not sufficiently mature in point of intelligence and experience to correctly apply or even to understand the rules of civilized warfare."

Under these circumstances, General Chaffee ordered Brigadier General Jacob H. Smith, U. S. Army, to command the 6th Separate Brigade and handle the situation on Samar. Lacking enough soldiers to form a full brigade, General Chaffee requested that Admiral Frederick Rodgers, Commander-in-Chief Asiatic Squadron, lend him some marines. Rodgers complied by sending Waller, with orders that read, "By direction of the senior squadron commander [Rodgers], you will assume command of a battalion of United States Marines for duty on the island of Samar." The Navy left the conduct of operations to Waller's estimation of the situation. The battalion of 315 marines embarked aboard the USS *New York* at Cavite on 22 October and landed at Catbalogan, Samar, on 24 October.

Waller, unlike Connell, took a more realistic view of the situation on Samar. The day before debarkation, Waller issued explicit orders to his officers concerning relations with the natives and rules of engagement:

". . . Place no confidence in the natives, and punish treachery immediately with death. . . .

". . . Allow no man [marine] to go . . . anywhere without his arms or ammunition. . . .

". . . All males who have not come in and presented themselves by October 25th will be regarded and treated as enemies. It must be impressed on the men that the natives are treacherous, brave and savage. No trust, no confidence, can be placed in them. . . .

". . . The men must be informed of the courage, skill, size and strength of the enemy. WE MUST DO OUR PART OF THE WORK, AND WITH THE SURE KNOWLEDGE THAT WE ARE NOT TO EXPECT QUARTER. . . ."

Waller viewed the situation as open combat governed by the rules of war. The populace would have to register with the marines or be considered combatants. Waller's orders to his officers were posted and the Naval high command took no exception to them, nor did General Smith, Waller's immediate senior. Waller's orders were within the limitations of General Order No. 100 of 1863 dealing with irregular warfare, which stated that if enemy units gave no quarter and became treacherous upon capture, it was lawful to shoot anyone belonging to that captured unit.

General Smith's orders to Major Waller upon arrival at Samar have allowed some historians to give Waller an out. These orders, stated orally and in unsigned note, were subsequently proven at Smith's own court-martial: "I want no prisoners. I wish you to kill and burn. The more you kill and burn, the better it will please me. . . . [T]he interior of Samar must be made a howling wilderness. . . ."

Some historians feel that Waller was only following the direct orders of his immediate senior officer. But, as testimony in General Smith's court-martial pointed out, Waller did not execute Smith's orders. Instead, Waller applied the rules of civilized warfare and the rules provided under General Order No. 100. Waller testified that he did not kill women or children and that he treated prisoners according to the rules of civilized warfare: "Always when prisoners came in and gave themselves up they were saved, they were not killed." In essence, Waller disobeyed Smith's direct orders, which refutes any claim that Waller was "just following orders." Instead, Waller's interpretation of Smith's orders demonstrated Waller's high moral courage and his effort to apply the rules of civilized warfare.

The marines' tactical area of responsibility was the southern half of Samar. Waller was relentless in his pursuit of the insurrectionists. He ran patrol after patrol, amphibious operations, a combined land and river attack on the insurrectionists' camp on the Sohoton Cliffs, and small raiding expeditions. The keys to Waller's successes were the flexibility of his tactics, his endurance, and the stamina of his men. Within a few months, the operations were beginning to take effect, but marine casualties were also frequent. The insurrectionists, armed with the Krag-Jorgensen rifles taken from Company C, bamboo cannon, and bolo knives, were a formidable foe for the marines. While running combat operations, Waller, always alert for any treachery, at the same time attempted to register the natives and pacify the towns. Waller's successes on Samar were heralded throughout the military command in the Philippines.

General Smith, desiring to get better communications on Samar, ordered Waller to scout a telegraph route from Lanang on the east coast to Basey on the west coast. On 28 December 1901, Waller, with 60 marines, two native scouts, and 33 native bearers, started from Lanang and headed into the interior of the Samar jungles, an area where few natives and no foreigners had ever gone. Within a few days, almost all the men were suffering from fever and other afflictions, as cited by Waller: ". . . Water sores [which] began to form where the clothing bore on the skin were developing rapidly . . . we suffered from sores caused by being constantly wet; also from the cuts made by the thorns and from bites of leeches. All these places festered and made very uncomfortable sores. . . ."

The terrain was exceedingly difficult. The marines were running out of food and began to starve. By 3 January 1902, Waller decided to split his unit. Leaving behind with Captain David D. Porter, U.S. Marine Corps, the bulk of the unit who were unable to march any farther, Waller set out for Basey with 14 marines and arrived there on 6 January 1902. With total disregard for his own health, Waller personally led a relief column the next day in an attempt to reach Porter. For nine days he searched for Porter without success.

Porter, in the meantime, had three options: to attempt to follow Waller, whose trail was unsure; to stay where he was and perish; or to attempt to backtrack to Lanang. He chose to backtrack. Leaving the sick and dying marines with First Lieutenant A. S. Williams, Porter headed for Lanang with seven marines and six natives. Hampered by torrential rains, Porter arrived at Lanang on 11 January. He immediately sent out a relief column to pick up his own stragglers and to rescue Williams' command.

Williams' fate was disastrous. Realizing that if he stayed where he was, he and his command were sure to die, he decided to head back to Lanang. His men, "so nearly dead from starvation and exposure that they began to crawl," slowly perished along the way. One marine went insane. By 18 January, when the relief column reached Williams, ten marines had died. In addition, the natives had mutinied.

Waller had used the natives as bearers of food and supplies on the march, but had no confidence in the allegiance of the natives to the marines and kept ever mindful of an attempted attack, which he and his officers had taken precautions to prevent. Natives could use a bolo knife only to help the marines hack through the jungle; every evening the knives were collected and counted. The natives were kept spread along the column with marines and away from the rifles. At night and during rest periods, the natives were huddled in one area and watched over by marines. The natives were apparently playing a waiting game; they would wait until the marines were in a weakened state, steal their weapons or overpower them one at a time, and kill them. First, a native called Victor stole Waller's bolo at night while Waller was asleep. Before the native could turn on him, Waller awoke, drew his pistol, and seized the bolo. Upon reaching Basey, Victor was imprisoned and became the first native to be shot by the firing squad on 20 January. Waller testified that Victor was revealed to be the "'Captain Victor' that notorious and infamous captain of insurrectos, who was of the detail from Basey in the Balangiga massacre." Second, the natives with Lieutenant Williams' group became rebellious. Williams testified that, ". . . the mutinous demeanor of the natives caused me daily fear of massacre." Third, the natives were hiding food and supplies from the marines while keeping themselves well nourished and securing food for themselves on the march.

Finally, there was open rebellion against Williams' party. Three of the natives, armed with a bolo knife, attacked and wounded Williams. The other natives watched while Williams managed to fight off the attack. These natives were put under arrest when the marines reached Lanang. It was this group of natives that was shot by the firing squad on 20 January, charged, in Day's words, with "treason in attempting to kill Lieutenant Williams, with treason in general, theft, disobedience and . . . general mutiny." Waller erred at this point by not putting the charge in writing. Williams' men were in such a weakened condition that they could offer little assistance at the time of the incident. Soon after the incident, Williams formulated several plans to kill the natives, but doubted the strength of his weakened men. He also felt that it was better to refer the incident to his commanding officer, Major Waller.

On 20 January, the U.S. gunboat *Arayat* arrived at Basey from Lanang and offloaded the native prisoners. After being briefed by his officers and noncommissioned officers, all of whom recommended execution, Waller ordered the natives to be shot. Waller stated:

> . . . The reports of the attempted murder of the men and other treachery of the natives, the whole plot being unmasked, caused me to hold an inquiry and consult with my officers. The population of the town was hostile at the time. . . . Using my own judgment, and fortified by the opinion of the officers and men, I had the guilty men shot, releasing the innocent. The power exercised was mine by right as commanding the district. It seemed to the best of my judgment, the thing to do at the time. I have not had reason to change my mind.

Thus the technical reason for Waller's court-martial was not so much that he shot the natives, but that the shootings were summary. This leads one to believe that Waller was charged with the wrong offense.

Waller felt that he had acted within the framework of General Order No. 100, which did not call for a trial of the accused, and within his authority as a district commander, although this was disputed by the Judge Advocate General. The real issue was that the responsibilities of a district commander in the Philippines were never clearly defined and that the tactical situation necessitated his actions. On 22 January, Waller, seeing no wrong in his actions, sent this message to General Smith: "It became necessary to expend eleven prisoners. Ten who were implemented [*sic*] in the attack on Lt. Williams and one who plotted against me."

On 19 February the marine battalion on Samar received orders to return to Cavite and arrived there 29 February. The unit returned to a welcoming home salute and party, but there was something else in store for Major Waller—a murder charge. Waller tended to place much of the blame for the court-martial on Lieutenant Day, although not during the trial or in public; during the trial he assumed full responsibility for his actions. Day, who was the battalion's adjutant and had not gone on the expedition, had boasted about his part in the execution. It was a bit of "action" for him. Waller stated after the trial in an after-action report, ". . . The charge was largely instigated by the vain boastfulness of one of the officers of my battalion."

Waller's court-martial lasted from 17 March to 12 April 1902. The court consisted of seven Army officers and six Marine Corps officers and was headed by Army Brigadier General William H. Bisbee, "a stalwart old Indian fighter." Waller argued that, because he had never been detached from his marine unit, an Army court had no jurisdiction over him. The court denied Waller's lack of jurisdiction claim, then proceeded to the specific number of natives executed and the issue of Waller's guilt or innocence. General Smith was called to testify concerning the orders he had issued to Waller prior to the Samar campaign. (His testimony later instigated his own court-martial.)

Waller could have made excuse for his actions by saying that he was injured and lying in a hospital when he issued his orders. But instead, he stood committed to his actions: "... As the representative officer responsible for the safety and welfare of my men, after investigation and from the information I had, ... I ordered the eleven men shot. I thought I was right then, I believe now I was right. Whatever may happen to me I have the sure knowledge that my people know, and I believe the whole world knows, that I am not a murderer."

The court voted eleven to two for acquittal. Headed by an old troop leader and field officer, General Bisbee, it must have weighed the tactical situation and the mitigating factors involved in the case. Many of the court's officers had been through guerrilla warfare in both the Philippines and the American West. It seems that they, as Waller's peers, realistically assessed the factors influencing Waller's decisions. Later, in the United States, the Army Judge Advocate General dismissed the entire case as illegal, agreeing that a Marine Corps officer was not subject to an Army court.

The type of combat fought on Samar was some of the most brutal of the Fil-American War. When his native bearers turned on him and his officers, Waller guided his actions on doctrinal orders, the rules of civilized warfare, and an estimation of the tactical situation as he saw it. Upon consultation of his officers and noncommissioned officers, Waller had the natives executed.

The decisions and conduct of men during war or in trying environments may seem questionable to outside observers, but seldom questionable to the participants at the time. The purpose of a court-martial is to obtain justice by one's military peers. The officers of the court were little affected by public opinion and high-level politics. The overwhelming majority of the court agreed with the opinions of Waller's officers and the accused, and acquitted Waller for his actions.

Waller's court-martial had effects on its participants and on the country as a whole. It informed the American public as to the type of warfare that was taking place in the Philippines. Even to its most ardent supporters, "benevolent assimilation" had its limits. The trial frustrated American civilian authorities and their attempts to implement their policies in the Philippines.

On 21 April 1902, General Smith was brought to trial on the charge of "conduct to the prejudice of good order and military discipline" for orders issued to Waller at Samar. He was found guilty and was eventually forced to leave the service. Lieutenant Day was also court-martialed but, like Waller, was acquitted. Waller continued to serve in the Marine Corps with distinction. In 1910, the "outstanding troop leader of the period" was passed over for Commandant, probably because of his one blemish, the court-martial.

Another result was marine respect. For many years afterward, marine messes would stand whenever a "Samar battalion" officer was present and toast, "Stand, gentlemen, he served on Samar."

10 "I HAD TO LAUGH"

(Selection from *The Reminiscences of Captain Daniel Webb Tomlinson IV*)

CAPT Daniel W. Tomlinson, USNR (Ret.)

This oral history interview with a pioneer of naval aviation who served in the 1920s—an interview conducted, amazingly, in 1989—illustrates how courts-martial can relate to the problem of change in military organizations. Whenever this early Navy pilot crashed a plane, distant superiors ordered that he be brought up on charges. Military courts examined troubling events during a period of testing and tinkering in an emerging technology.

"I HAD TO LAUGH"

(Selection from *The Reminiscences of Captain Daniel Webb Tomlinson IV, U.S. Naval Reserve [Ret.]*) by CAPT Daniel W. Tomlinson IV, USNR (Ret.) (Naval Institute Press, 1985): 1-35–1-42.*

[…]

I wanted to learn to fly land planes. They had a couple of 150-power Hispano Jennies at the air station, so I contacted a pilot who could fly them. He took me around the island one afternoon. I made a landing, no problem. He said, "Tomorrow morning you take this plane and spend a couple of hours flying around. Get used to it."

---

* The interviews in this oral history are paginated separately: e.g., 1-35 refers to page 35 of interview 1.

So the next morning I took off. I didn't have to go just around the island this time. He said I could take a couple of hours. So I went out a little farther, circled around over Coronado, and looked down at my house. I was up about 1,500 feet. I looked around and thought, "There's my house down there." All of a sudden, the motor quit. I was scared fartless. The bay and the ocean were in sight. If you've got wheels under you, it is different. There was Olive Avenue in Coronado right below me. At least I could get the plane on the ground on Olive Avenue, and I did. I had to dive under some telephone wires. The street was a bit too narrow and took off each upper wing overhang on the trees. When I came to an intersection, there came a milk truck. Fortunately, there weren't any wires across this intersection. I was going pretty fast, really charging down Olive Avenue. I just hopped over the milk truck and landed on the other side. I had no brakes. I made a perfectly good landing, but I couldn't control the plane directionally, and the plane ground-looped over the curb between trees. The airplane wasn't too badly damaged. Actually, the station repaired it, and it was flying in about a week or ten days later.

The stuff hit the fan after that: "That crazy Tomlinson landing on Olive Avenue in Coronado." I forget the name of the captain who was in command of the air station. He said, "Young man, you've created an awful uproar over there. I'm going to have to put you under hack for five days." There was no question about the engine quitting, because what had happened was a common fault with this model Hispano. On the left bank, there was an air pump which was operated by one of the valve cams. There was a leather washer in the air pump. When that washer would dry up, the pump failed. You had to have air pressure on the gas tank to force the gas up to the carburetor, which was between the V in this Hispano motor. No question—the motor quit on me.

I went under hack for five days. A couple of weeks later, orders came from Washington to try me by general court-martial for failing to maintain altitude in accordance with Navy regulations. I had to laugh. As my counsel I got a smart sea lawyer. He also was one of the famous drunks at that time but sharp as a whip when he was sober. We had no trouble convincing the court that even Jesus Christ couldn't make it; the motor quit. He might have been able to walk on water, but I doubt if even He could fly without power. So I was acquitted. That took care of that, and I went back to duty.

By October I could fly pretty well. I could fly anything available. Art Gavin was assembly and repair at the air station, and he used me to test new airplanes that he'd assembled. He'd put one on the field, call me to fly it or check it for stability, controllability, and balance in order to see that it was okay. I took out a new VE-7 fighter. It was a nice airplane and handled beautifully, very much like an S.E.5.

[Interviewer]: Built by Vought.

Captain Tomlinson: Yes. I was flying around in this plane, and I'd put it through acrobatics—the loops and rolls—to make sure the wires and everything were all tight. I looked to my left, and there was a line formation. They were four Voughts similar to the one I was flying; they were from a fleet air squadron. I'd never seen a line-abreast formation before, so I flew closer to watch. I wanted to see what they'd do next, because at Pensacola all we'd ever flown was the old V formation.

I was off to the right of the leader and back, to give me a good vision of the formation. I thought, "Okay, they're over there; I'm over here. I can watch this maneuver." I saw the leader zoom a little. I recognized that as a signal, and I noticed the wingmen on the left side started to drop back. All number two had to do was drop back a little bit, and he was in position. Then number three had to drop back and go clear over on the right side of the leader.

[Interviewer]: To form an echelon.

Captain Tomlinson: To form a V. Apparently that was the signal to go back to V. I wasn't close to the formation. I was off to the right side; to this day I don't know exactly how far. But I was accused of attempting to join the formation. I was well away, witnesses said. I don't know for sure, but I felt I was a safe distance away. I saw the pilot who was flying in number-three position move over. He went right through the slipstream of pilot number two. I saw him wobble and drop back. Then he was still moving to the right on the same level at which the leader was flying. He hit the leader's slipstream, and I saw him wobble again. Then I lost sight of him.

The next thing I knew, I had no tail and my left wing was gone. He apparently swung wide over there, because about five feet of his left lower wing broke my fuselage off in back of the cockpit. His propeller just chewed off both upper and lower left wings. Later I found witnesses from North Island; a man on Point Loma; another by Dutch Flats, where they had flying fields; and another in San Diego. I had four witnesses who saw the whole thing. They testified that I was flying along by myself.

I wasn't out completely. I realized it was a helpless situation. We didn't have parachutes in those days. I took the seat cushion out from under my seat and held it in front of my face. That's the last thing I remember. When the plane crashed, the thing that saved me—and I've got a picture of it—was that the upper and lower right wings were still firmly attached to the stub of the fuselage, including the cockpit and engine section. The plane went into auto-rotation and fell like a spinning leaf, much slower than it would have in a dive or a vertical sideslip.

[Interviewer]: A vertical descent.

Captain Tomlinson: Practically a vertical descent but quite flat, auto-rotating due to the balance of the wreckage with the right wings firmly attached. There was an empty gas tank under my seat. The plane hit the filled-in ground out in front of the Marine barracks. The motor was four feet in the soft fill.

The other pilot's plane spiraled. He came out of the spiral, leveled off partially, and hit the ground at an angle of about 15 degrees. Unhappily, his head snapped forward when he hit. The control stick hit him in the forehead and killed him.

[Interviewer]: Otherwise he would have survived?

Captain Tomlinson: He should have, except for the control stick hitting his forehead. I've got a picture of it. All his controls were functional, even though his left lower aileron was damaged due to the wing tip striking my fuselage.

That really touched things off. I was unconscious for four or five days. Then a court of inquiry was held at the naval hospital a few days after I regained consciousness—before I had any opportunity to locate witnesses. They alleged I was attempting to join the formation and was an overtaking airplane and was responsible for the accident. The next thing I knew, here came orders from Washington again. They were not from a local command but from the Navy Department. They charged me with manslaughter and unlawfully trying to join this formation by being an overtaking aircraft.

Another strange thing was that there were four planes in the formation, and none of the other three people saw the collision.

I think the trial was in January, as soon as I got out of the hospital. My family, of course, was scared stiff, and so was I. I got in touch with the son of my great-uncle, Rear Admiral [Charles Russell] Train. By that time his son, Russell Train, was a captain in the Navy, on duty in the Navy Department. He recommended as my counsel a commander who was on duty at San Diego at that time. He had been on the Adjutant General's legal staff in Washington.

By that time, I was able to get around and pass the word. I needed witnesses who saw the actual collision. Today I can't tell you just how I made contact with these witnesses who saw the accident.

[Interviewer]: The four witnesses.

Captain Tomlinson: There were four. Anybody with any sense, just looking at the pictures of the wreckage, should have been able to see that to accuse me of being an overtaking plane was absurd. I was acquitted.

I might as well put this in now. Five or six years later, at a cocktail party in San Diego, one of the officers who was a member of the court came up to me. He said, "I want to tell you something. You know, except for one vote, you would have received a full and honorable acquittal," which apparently takes a unanimous vote. It was the senior medical officer on the court-martial; he at that time was a full commander. He was the one who tried to turn me down medically in San Diego in 1920, and he still hated aviators!

11 "MURDER"

Maj Edwin N. McClellan, USMC

A problem that came up repeatedly during the twentieth century involved the limits of military jurisdiction over members of the armed forces. When is a soldier, sailor, or Marine within reach of a court-martial, and when do his crimes fall outside the authority of the military? The answers to this often-asked question were sometimes quite surprising. This article, written in the 1920s, uses offensive and now-anachronistic language about ethnic identity, but offers an important example of a contest over justice and jurisdiction.

"MURDER"

By Maj Edwin N. McClellan, USMC, U.S. Naval Institute *Proceedings* (January 1926): 95–102.

A shot rang out sharply and echoed back from the green western hills beyond Peking in Cathay. Yung Wang, a Chinese field coolie, slumped across his hoe, his face registering dumb surprise rather than pain. The corporal of marines who had fired the fatal shot shortly thereafter found himself incarcerated in the Chinese gaol just inside the Chien Men Gate, whence he was taken and confined in the marines' brig in the shadow of the Tartar City Wall. The coolie died. The corporal was charged with murder, and a naval general court-martial was convened to try him. Captain Ecks, of the Marine Corps, was judge advocate and Captain Wye, of the same corps, consented to defend the accused. [...]

The accused realized the hopelessness of his cause. He had aimed and fired the shot at the now dead Yung Wang, as he worked in the field five miles beyond the Peking Legation walls. The corporal bared his soul to counsel. "The Chinks aren't humans," he explained. "I saw that funny figure in the field. It looked just like a blue rabbit and I could no more resist the temptation to fire at it than I could when I was out hunting. Why," continued the accused, "out at the Rifle Range the Chinks pick lead out of the earthen butts right under the targets while we are firing and occasionally we took a potshot at them, the same as we used to do at the monkeys jumping around in the trees back of the targets at Maquinaya near Olongapo in the Philippines."

But "irresistible impulse" at its best is no defense before a naval court-martial, so the accused would have pleaded guilty and had it over with—the quicker the better. But his counsel was wiser than his generation and certainly more hopeful than the accused. He was a neophyte of the naval legal profession who seemingly was committed to the theory that the object of a general court-martial is "not justice but a verdict." Environment and present conditions are the causes which produce this class. At any rate counsel solemnly advised the depressed accused as follows:

"When Captain Ecks, the judge advocate, tells you to stand up and reads the charge and specification to you and then asks you if you are guilty to the specification, don't say a word but take the paper I will hand you and read to the court what is typewritten on it. Are you sure of what I want you to do?"

"I will do as you say, sir, but there doesn't seem much use of doing anything at all," replied the corporal.

"Do what I say, anyway, and trust me," said Captain Wye.

And so the accused was arraigned—"Guilty or not guilty?" Looking over toward Captain Wye, the corporal received a paper from which he read to the court as follows: "Before pleading to the general issue I desire to enter a plea denying that this general court-martial has jurisdiction to try me on the charge of murder as alleged in the specification."

Counsel did not desire to make any remarks and the judge advocate in most convincing manner informed the court that if the crime of murder is committed outside the territorial jurisdiction of the United States, within a foreign country, naval general courts-martial have jurisdiction to try and punish the offender with death. At the conclusion of his remarks the judge advocate referred the court to certain laws, *Naval Courts and Boards*, and *Naval Digest*. His duty was admirably performed. All this, however, drew no reply from Captain Wye. He appeared to have lost interest in the point entirely. Indeed, what reply could he make to the affirmative and apparently adequate mandate of the Navy Law Book which, owing to its approval by the Secretary of the Navy, had the weight of regulations.

Boredom and a spirit of tolerant resignation tinged with superior wisdom were written upon the faces of the members as the president drawled out—"Court's cleared!" Forty-seven seconds later, by the wrist watch of Captain Wye, court was opened and the president announced: "Plea of the accused overruled!"

The corporal, of course, pleaded not guilty, and he was convicted and sentenced to ten years at hard labor. At the conclusion of the trial Captain Wye, as counsel, forwarded a brief to the convening authority requesting that he consider it in reviewing the record and that the brief be forwarded with the record. The request was granted.

The convening authority approved the proceedings, findings, and sentence, and in due time the record and brief arrived in the Office of the Judge Advocate General. Not long after, the accused was transferred to Mare Island as a general court-martial prisoner.

The Judge Advocate General, after careful consideration of the record and the brief, informed the Secretary of the Navy that, in his opinion, the general court-martial possessed adequate jurisdiction, and that the proceedings, findings, and sentence were legal. Captain Wye was so informed.

This final decision of the Department had been anticipated by Captain Wye and he had written to a lawyer-friend, practicing in San Francisco, requesting him to take an interest in the case. This lawyer instituted *habeas corpus* proceedings with the result that the corporal was released from confinement by order of the federal judge. What the judge said was brief, but to the point, and follows:

A naval court-martial is a body of special, inferior, and limited jurisdiction. It has no power or jurisdiction which laws have not conferred upon it. Jurisdiction, of a limited nature, concerning the crime of murder, is conferred by law in these words: "If any person *belonging to any public vessel* of the United States commits the crime of murder without the territorial jurisdiction thereof, he may be tried by court-martial and punished with death."

Thus in order for the crime of murder to come within the jurisdiction of a naval court-martial the specification must truthfully allege that the offense was committed by a person "belonging to" a public vessel of the United States and that it was committed "without the territorial jurisdiction" thereof.

In this case the specification alleges that the accused corporal committed the crime of murder beyond the territorial jurisdiction of the United States but not that he belonged to a public vessel thereof. On the contrary the specification affirmatively alleges that he belongs to the Marine Detachment of the American Legation, which, the court taking judicial notice, is not a public vessel.

At the date Congress conferred limited jurisdiction to naval courts-martial over the crime of murder, naval personnel, not belonging to public vessels, was not serving ashore in foreign countries, nor did Congress anticipate that many years later such personnel would serve in China, Cuba, Nicaragua, Mexico, Haiti, Santo Domingo, Azores, France, Germany, Belgium, the British Empire, and other states.

If public policy demands that the jurisdiction of naval courts-martial be extended to include the crime of murder when committed without the territorial jurisdiction of the United States by naval personnel "not belonging to any public vessel," Congress should be asked to confer it.

That was the opinion of the federal judge. In brief, the upshot of the whole matter was that the naval court-martial did not possess jurisdiction to try this corporal on the charge of murder and the court set him free on *habeas corpus* proceedings.

News filtered back to Peking. The astuteness of Captain Wye became the subject of much comment.

12 "I JUST DON'T LIKE THE UNIFORM CODE"

(Selection from *The Reminiscences of Rear Admiral George W. Bauernschmidt*)

RADM George W. Bauernschmidt, USN (Ret.)

This oral history interview covers two significant moments of change in the Navy: First, the appearance of women in uniform during World War II (known then as WAVES, for Women Accepted for Volunteer Emergency Service), and second, the later replacement of the Articles for the Government of the United States Navy with the Uniform Code of Military Justice. In both cases, the interviewee uses the language of paternalism to describe pre-UCMJ naval justice: an officer taking care of the people who served under his command.

"I JUST DON'T LIKE THE UNIFORM CODE"

(Selection from *The Reminiscences of Rear Admiral George W. Bauernschmidt, U.S. Navy [Retired]*) by RADM George W. Bauernschmidt, USN (Ret.) (Naval Institute Press, 1969–70): 5-213–5-214, 6-267–6-269.

[...] Meantime, the 500 WAVES had also arrived, and they filled a big gap and did excellent service. However, it fell my job to hold mast on those WAVES who committed minor breaches of discipline. As I held mast, the senior WAVE officer always stood in back of me and breathed down my neck. After some sessions such as this, she came to me one day and said, "Captain, I've been observing you holding mast [as if I hadn't known it], and you show every evidence of having successfully raised a couple of daughters. I like very much the way you hold mast."

Well, that was one point of view. My wife happened to come out that evening to pick me up, and I was holding mast at the end of the day. Maude had already arrived, and she said, "What'll I do?"

I said, "Sit over in the corner behind a newspaper. The girls are so nervous they won't even know you're in here." Which she did.

On the way home, I got another point of view. Her remark was quite succinct. She said, "You certainly are a sucker for tears." [. . .]

[. . .] I also deplore the advent into the Navy of the Uniform Code of Military Justice. It was needed for the Army. It wasn't needed for the Navy. I have said many times that if I were innocent, I'd rather be tried by naval court-martial. If I were guilty, I'd rather be tried by a civilian-oriented court, with all of the legal hocus-pocus that provides endless loopholes for delay and acquittal or dismissal of the charges.

Under the old system every officer had his personal copy of Courts and Boards. They were comparatively simple. There was the minimum of material for the shyster type of legal objection. You were given rules of evidence, and you followed them. And that was it. But to be really constantly familiar with the provisions of Courts and Boards, you had to take an exam on them every time you went up for promotion. So you were always reading both the Navy Regulations and Courts and Boards. You were familiar with the areas which constituted offenses, and you were familiar with legal rights and responsibilities. I felt that it was a much healthier arrangement than that which we have now. Also, the Uniform Code of Military Justice did away with much of the commanding officer's authority to administer justice.

That, to my mind, worked distinctly to the disadvantage of the enlisted man. For the most part, a young man coming before a commanding officer gets rapped on the knuckles, very much as a commanding officer might rap his own children, and then just turned loose with his record unimpaired. Now the best the commanding officer can do is order a court-martial of one category or another and mess up the enlisted man's record. Possibly, it's because times have changed and officers are no longer of the breed that was represented by the term "officers and gentlemen," and they need some form of punishment, but I don't believe that.

The Uniform Code of Military Justice provides that officers may now be fined. Before, they could only be fined by courts-martial. I think that's wrong. Well, I just don't like the uniform code. I operated under it for a while, and I found it very difficult to administer. I had young men in my command—this was later, when I was at Pearl—who committed offenses for which I could have given two days' bread and water under the old system, and they'd never have come back. Under the new system, I either had to turn them loose or give them a court-martial. For the latter they got counsel, and counsel, inevitably, in talking to the man and providing for his defense, created in his mind the belief that, after all, he's being mistreated: "This is all wrong. I shouldn't be here before the court. I should be acquitted." So he acquires a shield of injured innocence. The result is that he goes out and commits another offense, and then another one. The first thing you know, he's getting clobbered with a big court, whereas if he'd gotten two days' bread and water to begin with, that would have been the end of it.

13 "NAVAL WAR-TIME DISCIPLINE"

VADM J. K. Taussig, USN

An important essay published just before the final year of World War II, this article describes a crisis in naval justice brought on by the rapid wartime growth of the armed forces—and, for example, the arrival in uniform of a subculture of sailors who were happy to be thrown out of a service they wanted to escape, leading to the realization among naval leaders that a bad conduct discharge was sometimes a reward. Navy leaders examining military justice reform during the war were caught in that classic dilemma of trying to figure out if they could rebuild a car while they were driving it.

"NAVAL WAR-TIME DISCIPLINE"

By VADM J. K. Taussig, USN, U.S. Naval Institute *Proceedings* (July 1944): 859–65.

The rapid war-time growth of the Navy, Marine Corps, and Coast Guard to a personnel total exceeding three million has created a discipline problem far different from that existing in times of peace. Prior to Pearl Harbor, our personnel were all volunteers, all of whom were subject to a careful process of selection, and most of whom enlisted with the intention of making whichever service they joined their lifetime Work. Their training was long and thorough, resulting in a knowledge and understanding of the traditional naval spirit in which discipline is a very large part. Generally speaking, separation from the service provided a simple means of dealing with the relatively few who were unable or unwilling to profit by this training. Now, however, a large proportion of the personnel are either inductees or volunteers who enlisted in the Navy, Marine Corps, or the Coast Guard, as the case might be, solely for the reason that they preferred to select a branch of service rather than to await induction without choice in the matter. In either case, these men have no intention of remaining in the service when the war is over. A large majority are young men entirely unaccustomed to the rigors of discipline, and the complete indoctrination of whom can be achieved only gradually. Moreover, the standards for admission to the service are lower, and those of relatively inferior caliber create a problem disproportionate to their number. Lastly, separation from the service, however satisfactory a solution in aggravated disciplinary cases in peace time, simply does not work when a war is being fought.

Many of our enlisted personnel have the attitude, all too prevalent in the general public, that the disregard and evasion of laws and regulations are to be expected and are not too censurable. Unfortunately, many officers have, in the past, taken this same attitude with respect to the commission of military offenses, such as absence without leave or absence over leave. They have considered disobedience of orders of this form to be inevitable and corrective action neither indicated nor possible. The expansion in untrained personnel together with the attitude of both officers and men towards infractions of discipline created a problem which was not fully foreseen and, in any event, one for which an adequate solution was not developed. A year and a half after Pearl Harbor the situation had assumed proportions that brought about an awakening to the necessity for immediate remedial action.

The failure to appreciate that with the great influx of new undisciplined recruits the commission of the so-called military offenses would increase at least proportionately resulted in an overcrowding of such prisons, brigs, and disciplinary barracks as were available. In addition, there was a marked slow down in the turning of the wheels of justice. An immense amount of work both administrative and clerical was required in the preparation of recommendations and orders for trial, drawing of charges and specifications, trial of cases, preparation of records, and last, but not least, in the procedure for review either required by law or established by policy.

Many officers were, and some still are, of the opinion that there are too many more important matters connected with the fighting of this war to worry about absenteeism and the causes therefor. This attitude is due, of course, to a lack of understanding of the effect this absenteeism is having on the war effort. Perhaps when the service at large has an appreciation of the situation, and what has been done and is continuing to be done to improve it, there will be an awakening that will materially assist those who are specifically charged with the responsibility of maintaining discipline. This article is written in the hope that the information set forth will result in a better understanding of this very important disciplinary problem.

There are now approximately three million men in the Navy, Marine Corps, and Coast Guard. It has been estimated that about 5 per cent of this number are potential delinquents in the sense that they, because of early training and environment, intelligence, psychological pattern, and other factors will be prone to the commission of offenses. The majority of disciplinary infractions will occur among this relatively small, but numerically large, group of approximately 150,000 men. Although statistical data are not available, our studies indicate that an average of approximately 50,000 men are at all times absent from their duty or station without leave or over leave, or are in confinement in prisons, brigs, or disciplinary barracks serving sentences of confinement or awaiting disciplinary action. In other words, we are annually losing about 18 million man days of what might be effective fighting service. And this does not tell the whole story, because these losses are greatly augmented by the personnel required to administer the disciplinary system and to officer and man prisons, brigs, and disciplinary barracks where an average of not less than 15,000 men are in confinement. To express in another way the effect on the war effort of this loss of man days, it may be pointed out that it at least equals the man days required for the construction of one of our largest battleships. No attempt is made here to estimate the monetary loss involved.

The seriousness of the loss of man days due to infractions in discipline was brought home to the authorities by the overcrowding of the facilities for handling prisoners, and by disciplinary procedures ill-adapted to war-time conditions which resulted in a disproportionate number of men being held in confinement awaiting final action. An investigation and study of these conditions revealed that in the case of men tried by general courts the average time between the recommendation for trial and the commencement of the sentence was over three months, and that men were not infrequently confined for from four to six months awaiting sentence. In the meantime, the pay of these offenders accrued on the books with the result that they, when restored to duty after confinement, received $200 or more in a lump sum, considerable temptation to the weak and irresponsible ones to err again.

By the spring of 1943 the need for a revision in the procedures in court-martial cases had become obvious. The Secretary of the Navy, in June, 1943, requested Mr. Arthur Ballantine, an eminent New York lawyer, "to prepare and submit as promptly as practicable a report on the organization, methods, and procedure of naval courts with recommendations, if found warranted, of possible improvement in procedure and practices that will facilitate the satisfactory handling of the largely increased volume of cases handled by such courts." Associated with him in the preparation of this report was Mr. Noel T. Dowling, a professor in the School of Law of Columbia University, who during the last war held a commission in the Army Judge Advocate Corps.

After three months of study during which many officers with experience in disciplinary problems and procedures were consulted, Mr. Ballantine, on September 24, 1943, submitted his report to the Secretary of the Navy containing a number of specific recommendations. However, a preliminary recommendation with respect to the decentralization of authority for ordering general courts-martial was submitted in July. The substance of this recommendation was to grant the Commandants of Naval Districts in the continental United States the same authority to convene general courts-martial as that held by

Commanding Officers of certain forces afloat or beyond the continental limits of the United States. Mr. Ballantine pointed out that the delegation of such authority would mean "the saving of at least sixty per cent of time now consumed due to the present centralization of such authority in Washington, a saving which would aggregate considerably over 500,000 man days a year." It was stated that there were then approximately 750 recommendations for general courts-martial coming to the Secretary of the Navy each month from the various districts, and that this number was on the increase; that, except in limited cases such as by authority of a Commander of a Sea Frontier, no case could be submitted to a general court-martial in the continental United States even where there was a "permanent" court, without the approval of the Secretary of the Navy; that recommendations for trial had to come from the field to Washington; that they had to be cleared through both the Judge Advocate General's office and the Bureau of Naval Personnel; that specifications had to be drawn by the Judge Advocate General and returned to the field; that no sentence was carried into execution until it had been reviewed in Washington by both JAG and BuPers, and, as approved, included in an enbloc letter authorizing promulgation of the sentence; and that each case had to make two round-trips to Washington before the sentence could be put into execution.

The Secretary immediately adopted this recommendation and by appropriate authorizations empowered Commandants of all Naval Districts in the continental United States to convene general courts-martial. The beneficial effects of this action began to be immediately realized in a gradual reduction of the elapsed procedure time in general court-martial cases. [. . .]

The only recommendation with respect to sentences of general courts-martial is: "*Naval Courts and Boards* should be revised to grant general courts-martial larger powers and responsibilities for fixing sentences."

The approval and adoption of this recommendation would result in a basic change in policy having far-reaching effects. It is therefore of interest to the service to learn the reasons for this recommendation. In the discussion of this subject it is pointed out that a study of 1,600 cases cleared through the Office of the Judge Advocate General during a three-month period showed that over three quarters of the sentences adjudged were substantially mitigated in the process of review. Under existing procedure, it is the duty, as prescribed in *Naval Courts and Boards*, of the court in all cases of conviction, "to adjudge a punishment adequate to the nature of the offense." At the same time, it is the privilege of the members of the court individually to "recommend the person convicted as deserving of clemency" and to state on the record their reasons for so doing. Clemency, however, "is to be exercised only by the reviewing authorities, who are expressly clothed with the power to remit or mitigate punishment." Moreover, the courts are admonished not to "presume upon the prerogative of the reviewing authority in exercising clemency"; for such action, so it is declared, "would be in effect, a reflection upon the judgment of the reviewing authority." Somewhat inconsistently, courts are expressly authorized to receive matter in mitigation for the purpose of lessening "the punishment to be assigned by the court."

It is pointed out that the British system furnishes a sharp contrast in this respect. Their *Manual of Naval Law and Court Martial Procedure* states:

> In awarding sentences, the court should take into consideration the former services and any other claims which the accused may lay before them, with a view to his being dealt with more leniently. It is objectionable for a court to award a sentence and then to recommend a prisoner to the favorable consideration of the Admiralty. Such a course throws a responsibility upon others which properly belongs to the court.

It is apparent that the eminent lawyers who made the study of our procedure consider the British method of awarding punishments better. They state that except in the matter of determining general policies governing punishments, the court is in the best position to fix sentences as it is the only place in the system where the man himself is actually under observation and appraisal. It was also noted that increase in the powers of courts to determine ultimate punishments might well be accompanied by a procedural change requiring the announcement of findings and sentences in open court at the conclusion of trial, as this would augment the sense of responsibility of the court, while the prompt public announcement of sentences should have a desirable deterrent effect.

This change in procedure, if adopted, will undoubtedly have a marked effect on the actions of general courts. There is no doubt but that, under the system which we have followed for years, members of courts have generally been unwilling to undergo the risk of criticism based on supposed inadequacy of sentence which is inherent in attempting to fix a just and final measure of punishment. The result has been that courts usually impose excessively severe sentences which are mitigated with monotonous regularity. Indeed, there is now considerable complaint throughout the service that mitigation of sentences by reviewing authorities has been indulged in to such a degree that sentences as finally approved are so mild as to be ineffective deterrents. My own opinion based on experience during the past eight months is that, with a short period of adjustment during which some guide issued by the Department should be available indicating appropriate sentences for similar offenses by all general courts, much benefit would accrue from adoption of the recommendations.

Mr. Ballantine made the following recommendations with respect to sentences by summary courts-martial.

> Summary Courts Martial should be empowered to adjudge sentences of greater severity than presently permitted and, in particular, to adjudge confinement and loss of pay for not more than six months.
>
> As a matter of policy, summary courts martial should not adjudge bad conduct discharges except where the offense involves moral turpitude or the accused is neither presently nor prospectively of any value to the Service.

The recommendation with respect to increasing the powers of summary courts-martial it is believed will receive universal approval by the service. At present, the maximum period of confinement which may be adjudged is two months, and the loss of pay shall not exceed three months. These limitations do not provide sufficient variation between summary and deck courts. In addition, they compel trial by general court-martial of many cases which could be tried by a summary court with somewhat larger powers. The Army counterpart of the summary court-martial, a "special court-martial," has the power to adjudge confinement not in excess of six months. The power to adjudge an increase in loss of pay will permit of adequate penalties without loss of man power.

There will probably be a divergence in opinion as to whether or not summary courts should cease to adjudge bad conduct discharges for purely so-called military offenses. In some commands the convening authorities have apparently indicated a desire for summary courts to include a bad conduct discharge in all cases involving absence over leave and absence without leave. In these cases the court usually adjudges an additional punishment of loss of pay. The convening authority then remits the bad conduct discharge on probation. This system has the advantage of eliminating the loss of man days which go with confinement, but its weakness is indicated by the rather prevalent practice of bringing the offender to trial again if probation is violated rather than merely carrying into execution the bad conduct discharge previously conditionally remitted.

The reasons for recommending the elimination of the bad conduct discharge for purely military offenses set forth in the Ballantine report may be paraphrased as follows: A bad conduct discharge is seldom an appropriate punishment in time of war. If executed, it results in a loss in man power while placing both the offender and the service in anomalous positions under the Selective Service Law. Moreover, if the offender is not reinducted in some branch of military service, the ultimate result is restoration to civil life with little difficulty in obtaining a safe and comparatively lucrative position. If the discharge is not executed, the offender necessarily escapes punishment except for possible loss of pay and extra police duties.

There is no doubt that there is a class of men, who, motivated by fear or otherwise, have sought to escape military service by "working for a B. C. D." As for a time there was a general service opinion that the best action was to get rid of these men, many bad conduct discharges were executed. This resulted in an increase rather than a diminution in the occurrence of offenses, as it became general knowledge that all one had to do in order to get fired was to be guilty of several unauthorized absences. We have now learned by experience that it is better for discipline in general to punish this class of offenders by loss of pay and confinement. It is noteworthy that the Army special court-martial has no power to adjudge discharge. [. . .]

With respect to sentences of Deck Courts the Ballantine report recommended: "Deck Courts should be empowered to adjudge sentences of greater severity than presently permitted and in particular to adjudge confinement and forfeiture of pay for not more than one month."

With respect to an increase of powers for deck courts it is pointed out that at present the powers are so circumscribed by limitations as to prevent the most effective use of the courts. In summary courts a proper distinction is made between mere confinement and solitary confinement on bread and water. Although confinement on bread and water is not generally looked upon with favor, a deck court must resort to this punishment to exercise its maximum powers since the same time limitation is applicable to ordinary confinement. As loss of pay is frequently more appropriate than confinement it would be desirable to increase the power of deck courts to adjudge loss of pay up to thirty days. Perhaps an even more substantial increase in the powers of deck courts would have been recommended if there was not an existing precedent for the proposed powers in the Army "summary court-martial"—a one-officer court corresponding to our deck court.

There is a difference of service opinion with respect to the appropriateness of solitary confinement on bread and water as a punishment. Some hold it to be outmoded by modern conditions. Others consider it the only effective punishment for a certain class of enlisted men. A discussion of the pros and cons of this question will be set forth later.

With respect to mast punishment, it was recommended that the Articles for the Government of the Navy be amended to permit commanding officers to inflict loss of pay not exceeding ten days. At present loss of pay is not authorized as a mast punishment in spite of the fact that it is frequently a most appropriate punishment. Aboard small ships confinement can be carried out only with considerable difficulty and often inconvenience to the crew. Therefore, the commander of such a vessel must of necessity often order a court in order that some punishment other than confinement may be adjudged. Many commanders of vessels resent the privilege granted by a deck court to a single officer, junior to themselves, and in consequence do not order such courts even in cases where loss of pay would be more appropriate than confinement. While it is believed that such action on the part of commanding officers is not justified, still it is done, and results in adjudging inappropriate punishments.

It is believed that concurrence in the recommendation to authorize loss of pay as a mast punishment will receive approval throughout the service and will if adopted result in improved discipline. There will be considerable sentiment to permit commanding officers to inflict as a mast punishment loss of pay exceeding ten days.

In concluding the report to the Secretary, Mr. Ballantine made these observations:

> This report deals with only one phase of the broad problem before the Navy. It is concerned with the question of a system for dealing with those charged with the commission of offenses. The problem presents two phases. First, there is the question of the causation of offenses. Second, there is the question of treatment of convicted offenders.

In explanation of this, Mr. Ballantine gives his impression that causation of offenses involving unauthorized absence should be the principal source of concern as approximately three-quarters of all court-martial cases involve this offense, while major military offenses and crimes are, in relation to the number and class of the naval population, gratifyingly rare.

With respect to the treatment of convicted offenders, it was suggested that benefit would be derived from the development of a plan to effect the speedy rehabilitation of the maximum possible number of offenders. The report further stated that naval prisons appear to place greater emphasis upon rehabilitation than the brigs. The value and effectiveness of rehabilitation programs are illustrated by the fact that the percentage of successful probationers restored to duty after confinement is greater in the case of men who were confined in prisons, usually for serious offenses, than in the case of men who were confined in brigs, usually for minor offenses.

The Ballantine report has received the careful consideration of the Secretary of the Navy and of the Bureaus and Offices directly concerned with the recommendations therein made. A number of additional suggestions have been advanced and variations proposed. As all of the recommendations and suggestions are more or less inter-related, and some of the most important would require Congressional action, it is unfortunately true that considerable delay is to be anticipated before they can be made effective. It is to be hoped that the delay will be held to a minimum in order that simplification of procedure and the improvement in discipline which may be expected to result from a more workable system of naval justice may be obtained as soon as possible.

14 "THE SINKING OF THE *INDY* & RESPONSIBILITY OF COMMAND"

CDR William J. Toti, USN

More than seven decades after it took place, the court-martial of Capt. Charles McVay remains controversial. McVay was tried after a Japanese submarine sank the ship he commanded, the heavy cruiser *Indianapolis*, in the last days of World War II. In 2000, after a long effort by survivors of the sinking, a congressional resolution—signed by President Bill Clinton—declared McVay to be "exonerated" despite his court-martial conviction. Note: The italic paragraphs at the beginning of this excerpt are from the opening photo caption for this 1999 article.

"THE SINKING OF THE *INDY* & RESPONSIBILITY OF COMMAND"

By CDR William J. Toti, USN, U.S. Naval Institute *Proceedings* (October 1999): 34–38.

The 1945 sinking of the heavy cruiser USS Indianapolis *(CA-35) by the Imperial Japanese submarine I-58 has been called the last, great naval tragedy of World War II. It is the stuff of legend: after delivering the atomic bombs to Tinian, the* Indy *was torpedoed, sinking in 12 minutes. At least 800 crew members survived the sinking and went into the water. On their rescue after five days, only 320 still were alive. Their stories have inspired three books, a movie, and perhaps yet another feature film.*

The Indy's *survivors [. . .] fought sharks, deprivation, and the elements, and now they fight to get their captain exonerated. Their commanding officer, Captain Charles B. McVay III, is the only captain ever to be court-martialed for having his ship sunk out from under him during time of war.*

[. . .]

The Court-Martial

The *Indy* controversy erupted in August 1945, just after the atomic bombs were dropped. The American public was outraged at the loss of more than 800 lives in the waning days of the war, and a Navy court of inquiry was convened to investigate. Its recommendation was that Captain McVay be court-martialed for hazarding his vessel by failure to zigzag, but Admiral Chester Nimitz disagreed and instead issued the captain a letter of reprimand. Admiral Ernest King later overturned Nimitz's decision and recommended a court-martial, which Secretary of the Navy Forrestal later convened.

In doing so, King intervened directly with the Secretary of the Navy to move forward with the court-martial in parallel with an investigation by the Inspector General (IG). But a court-martial is a trial, not an investigatory tool. If King's problem was simply a lack of information, why didn't he allow the Inspector General to issue his report before ordering the court-martial? Some believe it is because King was not satisfied that the IG's conclusions would support his decision to court-martial.

The Navy Judge Advocate General also was asked to review the referral. His response contained the curious statement that the charges included in the initial referral were "the only ones that can be supported," as if an agenda was at work to establish a greater foundation for prosecution. Whatever the truth, this statement certainly creates the perception that the Judge Advocate General was under direction to discover more charges to refer against McVay.

In the end, McVay was charged with two counts: suffering his vessel to be hazarded by failing to zigzag, and failure to order abandon ship in a timely manner. His counsel, reportedly hand-picked by King, had never argued a case in court before.

The court claimed that McVay was not being charged for any deficiency that led to the sinking of his ship. They made a strong case that the "*Indianapolis* was hazarded before she was ever detected by *I-58*, and would have been hazarded if she had never been detected by *I-58*." In essence, McVay could have been found guilty in a court-martial even if his ship had not been sunk. This is a meaningless legal distinction, however, since absent the sinking, there would have been no way for anyone to know that the vessel had been hazarded.

Hence, despite the fact that McVay was convicted only on the first count—for suffering his vessel to be hazarded by not zigzagging—there is no way to escape the fact that Captain McVay was court-martialed for having his ship sunk.

Put all these facts together, and it is understandable why most of the survivors believe that Admiral King was doing all he could to tilt the scales of justice against McVay. Even Admiral Nimitz later would say to one survivor that the entire affair involving the court-martial was a mistake and should never have happened.

Modern Perceptions and Recent Analysis

In more recent times, the story of the *Indianapolis* has become the stuff of legend. Unfortunately, the legend has in some cases overwhelmed the truth. For example, some of McVay's proponents opine that the Navy still is involved in some sort of cover-up, to hide the corporate Navy's culpability in the events that led up to the McVay court-martial. Any such notion obviously is ludicrous. No one on active duty today has any stake in a court-martial decision made in 1945. None of today's decision makers has any personal capital invested in this sequence of events. It would reflect poorly on none of them if they were to declare that McVay should not have been court-martialed almost 55 years ago. It is reasonable to conclude, therefore, that any contemporary declaration on the case is likely to be unbiased.

Which leads to the issue of recent statements on the subject by the Navy. The most recent review of the case was carried out by a Navy lawyer, Commander R. D. Scott, in 1996. The study is thoroughly researched, logically sound, and I will assume, legally correct. Nevertheless, some statements in the report show a lack of professional knowledge of the naval art, weaken the overall presentation, and unfortunately, lend credence to those who contend that the Navy still is engaged in shaping the argument against Captain McVay.

For example, in one of his footnotes, Commander Scott says, "The Navy has never challenged Captain McVay's uncorroborated account that he did not go down with his ship because he was swept over the side by a wave." The implication here is that it was McVay's duty to go down with his ship, a notion that is steeped in folklore but has no foundation in regulation or naval tradition. Worse, Scott implies here that Captain McVay—a man awarded the Silver Star for gallantry under fire, a man who spoke freely and honestly about the fact that he had not been zigzagging at the time he was torpedoed—was lying about something as trivial as how he found himself removed from his sinking ship. This is an implication that most of the survivors consider personally offensive, as do I.

Similarly, Scott is particularly critical of one recent book that recounts the story of the *Indianapolis*, *Fatal Voyage*. He proclaims this account "replete with melodramatic conjecture," but this has nothing to do with the veracity of the claims made by the author. In addition, Scott is anything but clinical in his analysis of the book, as when he describes author Dan Kurzman writing his missive with a "tortured pen."

Scott also writes that existing naval warfare publications directed commanding officers to zigzag anywhere a threat of submarine attack existed. By July 1945, however, the Imperial Japanese Navy barely existed, and the Philippine Sea where the *Indianapolis* was sunk was thought of as a backwater with an imperceptibly small probability of encountering the enemy. In addition, the *Indianapolis*'s routing order, which even Admiral Nimitz noted took precedence over the doctrine publication, gave McVay authority to zigzag "at his discretion." And last, McVay had been zigzagging throughout the daylight hours, and ordered a straight-line course only late in the evening, when the sky was obscured and visibility was poor. These facts weakened this line of reasoning so acutely that the prosecution never pursued a strategy of convicting McVay for failing to follow a lawful order.

Commander Scott also performs an assessment of the *I-58*'s attack, concluding that if the *Indy* had zigged at the time the submarine launched her torpedoes, the weapons would have missed. Notwithstanding the laws of probability that argue against this kind of fortuitous timing, combat is not a kid's game where everybody goes home after experiencing initial frustration. Even if the *I-58* had missed with the first salvo, she had other options at hand: she could have employed her Kaiten or suicide minisubmarines, which were guided; or she could have surfaced, repositioned, and pressed on the attack. Many of the U.S. Navy's most successful submarine commanders of World War II missed their initial attack but still achieved success. These men sank more than 4,000 ships, most of which were zigzagging. Scott exaggerates the difficulty that zigzagging would have presented to the commander of the *I-58*, and to propose that the *Indy* would have been spared had she zigged at time of fire weakens his overall argument.

In addition, Scott's assertion that zigzagging would have helped save the *Indianapolis* weakens his later statement that "whether zigzagging would have defeated submarine *I-58*'s targeting of *Indianapolis* was not the issue at Captain McVay's court-martial." If the efficacy of zigzagging was not the issue, why did the Navy's advocate in this matter spend so much effort trying to show that it would have been effective? Because he had to overcome the weight of evidence, most of which was provided by two men—the *I-58*'s captain, who was flown into Washington to testify against Captain McVay at his court-martial, and an experienced U.S. submarine commander. Even the prosecution's star witness, the CO of the attacking submarine, agreed that the *Indy* would have been sunk regardless of McVay's maneuvers.

The truth is that despite the Navy's claims to the contrary, McVay was convicted for having his ship sunk. And in the end, Commander Scott's assessment did little to assuage survivors' concern that their skipper continues to receive unjust treatment at the hands of the Navy.

The Responsibility of Command

Despite the weaknesses in Commander Scott's analysis of the McVay case, his conclusions essentially are correct. But he misses the real point. The question that should be asked is, If a ship with no antisubmarine warfare capability is sunk by a submarine in a war zone, is the commanding officer free from accountability?

The short answer is no. Regardless of legal wrangling, a commanding officer's responsibility, and his accountability, are absolute in matters that affect the safety of his ship. This tenet is founded in Section 5947 of Title 10, United States Code, which states: "All commanding officers . . . in the naval service are required . . . to take all necessary and proper measures, under the laws, regulations, and customs of the naval service, to promote and safe-guard . . . the physical well-being, and the general welfare of the officers and enlisted persons under their command or charge."

Or, as another Navy captain has said:

In the American Navy, the principle of accountability for the safety of one's crew derives directly from our long-standing tradition of the citizen-soldier. The Founding Fathers explicitly rejected the European tradition of a professional officer caste that puts its own stature and survival above that of troops forcibly drawn from the peasantry. Instead in our democracy, the military leader's authority over his troops was linked to a parallel responsibility to them as fellow citizens.

Accountability is a severe standard: the commander is responsible for everything that occurs under his command. Traditionally, the only escape clause was an act of God, an incident that no prudent commander could reasonably have foreseen. The penalties of accountable failure can be drastic: command and career cut short, sometimes by court-martial.

These factors favor the argument that a commander can and should be court-martialed for a failing that results in members of his crew being hurt or killed. Any deficiency in the ship is the CO's responsibility, even if he had no direct, causal relationship with the deficiency. This is because it is the commanding officer's responsibility—more than that, his duty—to ferret out and correct problems before they manifest in failure. If he fails at that task, there is no one to back him up.

Captain McVay was the son of an admiral, a second-generation Naval Academy graduate, and knew this well. He acknowledged his accountability on two separate occasions. First, after his rescue, he told the *New York Times*, "I was in command of the ship and I am responsible for its fate." And later, in his court-martial, he testified, "I know I cannot shirk the responsibility of command."

Captain McVay's ship was lost. He failed to take "all necessary measures" to protect his ship. And in our system of responsibility of command, it does not matter whether that action would have been effective—he should have tried. That is why he was found guilty.

Legal Correctness and Justice

So it seems that Captain McVay's conviction was legally correct. But was it just?

Out of several hundred ships sunk during World War II, Captain McVay was the only commanding officer ever to be court-martialed for having his ship sunk out from under him. Was every one of those other commanding officers faultless? Did every one of them take "all necessary measures" to protect his crew? Of course not. If those cases were subjected to the same level of scrutiny as the *Indy*, we probably would find some kind of failure in each event.

So why doesn't the Navy routinely court-martial commanding officers when their ships are sunk?

Consider how polite society responds to the death of a child. The parent sometimes has some degree of responsibility. Perhaps he left the child home alone. She let the child play too close to the street. Or they left matches in an accessible location. The parents could have prevented the tragedy—they might even be criminally negligent—but a humane society considers the impact of the tragedy on the accused, and understands that absent the grossest kind of malfeasance, the parent has suffered enough and should not be prosecuted. This is the concept of prosecutorial discretion. So it is with the sinking of a ship. The CO almost always can be found technically guilty of some form of negligence.

Indeed, a CO's responsibility is so vast that on almost any day, on almost any ship, any one of us could walk on board and find something for which the CO could be held legally culpable. But absent the worst kind of deliberate misconduct, COs are not routinely prosecuted, because pursuing this tenet too aggressively would result in an effusion of action tailored to prevent failure, rather than to pursue success.

Which brings us back to Captain McVay. Here was a man who, because of the unique and absolute nature of the responsibility of command, was culpable for the misfortune that befell his ship—the captain's own statements point to the fact that he understood this truth well. Despite that, there was nothing he could have done to prevent that misfortune, and he never should have been pro- secuted in the first place. The lesson here is that a decision can be legally correct and still be unjust.

It is worth pointing out that McVay's jury understood this paradox, and as a result, his sentence was light. He did not get demoted, as is commonly thought, but was merely set back in line for promotion. In addition, the members of the court-martial were unanimous in recommending that the reviewing authority exercise clemency. Why? Because they knew that, but for the grace of God, any one of them might have found himself in the same position as Captain McVay.

In fact, following the court-martial, Admiral King recommended setting aside even this token punishment. Secretary Forrestal accepted this recom- mendation, and McVay was promoted to rear admiral on retirement, consistent with the practice of the day.

An Epilogue

From 1945 on, McVay received hate mail every Christmas from a few persistent relatives of sailors killed on the *Indianapolis*. The support he received from fellow survivors did little to assuage his feelings of inadequacy and guilt, made worse by the fact that his conviction rendered him legally culpable for the deaths of his shipmates. On a gray day in 1966, he dressed in his Navy uniform, picked up a toy figure of a sailor, walked onto his front porch, put a handgun into his mouth, and pulled the trigger—yet another victim of a battle that claimed too many.

15 "LAYMAN TAKES ISSUE WITH LAWYERS"

CAPT J. M. Sheehan, USN (Ret.)

A growing consensus after World War II that military justice was a broken system resulted in a controversy that led to the creation of the new Uniform Code of Military Justice. But many experienced military officers disagreed. In this 1947 essay, a retired Navy officer described his personal experiences with courts-martial, arguing for the fairness of a justice system that many critics regarded as archaic and cruel.

"LAYMAN TAKES ISSUE WITH LAWYERS"

By CAPT J. M. Sheehan, USN (Ret.), U.S. Naval Institute *Proceedings* (September 1947): 1065–71.

During the last year or so, the public prints have contained a large number of very critical articles and commentaries upon the system of military justice employed by our armed forces. Many of these have been thoughtful, well-written pieces of work by experienced lawyers and law teachers, and some of their criticisms and suggestions toward improvement of the system possess a great deal of merit. On the other hand, many other of the writings appear to be rather ill-considered and ill-informed, and seem to arise principally from the traditional American attitude toward military authority, and also perhaps, from specific cases of seeming injustice, or from the resentment caused by unhappy personal experience.

Unfortunately there have been more than a few instances during the past great war which would appear to warrant the most scathing criticism and amply to warrant some drastic changes in our system of military justice. And yet, who can say with assurance that the system itself has been always and primarily at fault? The proper functioning of any system or apparatus ever devised by the mind of man depends mainly upon the particular human beings who operate it, and every day we can see about us the failures and disasters which take place despite the most careful planning and safeguards, and which can be attributed to but one thing; namely, the proverbial "human equation."

Never was this more evident, perhaps, than during the terrific stress and confusion of our vast war effort, where untoward things seemed bound to happen in spite of the best of skill and intentions on the part of those in charge, and where unfortunate things took place because the tremendous expansion of our armed forces unavoidably placed authority, at times, in hands ill-fitted to administer it properly.

"Ships are all right: it's the men in them," an elderly seaman once told Joseph Conrad, the great sea-writer, and there he uttered something that might apply fairly well in the present instance.

It is not intended to imply by all this that our system of military justice is above reproach, and that it is not susceptible to improvement, and considerable improvement perhaps, in some respects, even though intrinsically sound. Any system is always susceptible to improvement, and the changes for improvement should reflect to a great extent the changing ideas and standards of society as it progresses. But in regard to possible changes for improvement in our present court-martial procedures, it is noted that in their disquisitions most of the lawyer-critics, and even some of the most thoughtful, appear to be thinking with that thing always so baffling to the layman—the "legal mind"—and they seem to be not so much concerned with the better achievement of justice in our court-martial proceedings, as they are with fine points of legal ritual, and with the mechanics and legal virtuosity involved in confounding the opposite side and "winning the case." Some appear to deem it a grievous lack because the court-martial procedure tends to cramp the tactics so favored of trial lawyers, and because it has so little place for the oratory and histrionics they regard so highly. Some imply that by the nature of things, the defendant in a court-martial cannot obtain a fair trial, and their recommendations are mainly from this standpoint. They speak of "justice" only for the defendant, and they seem to overlook the fact that there is another side to the matter of justice. However, no matter how divergent the respective views of most of these lawyer-critics may be in other respects, they seem to be in grand accord upon the following:

(1) That our present court-martial procedures are archaic and inefficient, and they are inimical to the attainment of proper justice

(2) That the regular civil-court procedures are the very antithesis of this, and they stand out in shining contrast as the true embodiment of everything that's excellent in jurisprudence

(3) That the remedy for every alleged ill and shortcoming of our present court-martial procedure lies in the adoption of the analogous civil-court procedures in each instance.

It is at this point that one wonders if those well-meaning critics, despite the merit their comments may possess otherwise, have not placed themselves in a very vulnerable position, and one with which almost any observant layman could well take issue. [...]

During his years of service, and particularly while serving as member of a General Court-Martial at various times, the writer has never failed to be impressed by the dignity, simplicity, and intrinsic fairness of the required procedure. In such a court the rights of a defendant are just as well guarded as in any civil court, and usually much better, in fact. The Judge Advocate, as Prosecutor, has no political stake or prestige involved in the conviction of the accused; and while he must fully exert himself in carrying out his appointed task, the due rights of the accused are a part of his responsibility also. The protection of these rights is likewise a part of the bounden duty of the court, and it has been my personal experience that the court never hesitates to step in at any point where they may appear to be threatened.

Moreover, the very dignity and restraint required and insisted upon in a naval court undoubtedly contribute much to the achievement of proper justice in a case. In such court, the major issues and points of a trial usually are not allowed to become confused and beclouded by a deliberate welter of objections, arguments, the citing of bizarre and dubious precedents, and the sundry other maneuvers which seem to be regarded as smart courtroom strategy and tactics. There we see no unseemly brawling between rival attorneys, nor heated and sarcastic exchanges between attorney and judge, and other such things which certainly contribute little to the cause of justice. Above all, perhaps, the forensic fireworks and loud speeches, dripping with references to the Stars and Stripes, the Declaration of Independence, white-haired mothers, prattling babes, and such, and interlarded with more-or-less adroit appeals to various little prejudices: all these are rather conspicuous by their absence. Considering all this, the asserted superiority of the civil-court procedures seems hardly manifest; and while many of the practices cited above may be recognized and essential parts of the game to a trial lawyer, to imply that without such things our courts-martial do not and cannot achieve proper justice, seems somewhat on the preposterous side.

In regard to the allegation that our court-martial processes are "inefficient" in comparison with those of the civil courts, one wonders if those critics are actually serious in making such a statement.

As for just one aspect of "inefficiency"—surely we never see a court-martial postponed again and again through the maneuvers of high-priced legal talent, until probably after a year or so the public has forgotten the case; until prosecution witnesses have died or disappeared, and the memories of those still available are bound to be hazy; and until the State has no other course but to drop the case in futility, with the net result that a vicious criminal, perhaps, goes on his way scot-free and rejoicing. [. . .]

The rules governing naval courts-martial specifically enjoin that a witness be treated with due respect and dignity, and there is no doubt that this injunction is carefully observed. In the few instances this writer has seen where either the prosecutor or the defender began to exceed proper limits in his handling of a witness, an admonition from the court was quickly forthcoming, and it is certain that the cause of justice did not suffer in the slightest thereby.

On the other hand, many of us have seen, and perhaps some of us have experienced, the harassing, browbeating, and humiliation to which an honest citizen, endeavoring to tell an honest story, may be submitted in a civil court, and in which the end sought by such tactics is, of course, not the eliciting of proper and pertinent testimony, but instead merely the reduction of the witness to such a state of confusion as will best serve the interests of the examiner. [. . .]

One implication that seems to run through many of the critical commentaries, and which deserves comment here, is that existing court-martial procedures tend to stifle the efforts of a defense attorney, and prevent his giving his client the full benefit of his legal skill and knowledge. These critics appear to find the required orderly and restrained procedure of a naval court repressive and inadequate, and mainly, it seems, because it affords so little room or utility for the oratory, dramatics, and other tactics which they appear to regard as essential. Now certainly such things are not necessary to obtain justice in a naval court, and a skilled attorney can do an excellent job for his client there without them. The writer has seen this demonstrated many times, and, it should be especially noted, by certain civilian attorneys who undoubtedly were skillful trial lawyers otherwise, but also were accustomed to appearing in naval courts-martial for the defense. The quiet and restrained, but very effective manner in which these attorneys were wont to conduct their cases, and in which they managed to wring every possible beneficial point out of the evidence and proceedings, was usually quite impressive.

They served their clients well, won for them every possible advantage, and yet conformed to the required procedures with no apparent difficulty or sense of hindrance. By this it would seem that our court-martial procedures are not so unduly repressive, and not such an impediment to the proper efforts of a defense attorney, as these earnest critics would have us believe.

16 "THE COMMANDING OFFICER AND THE NEW UNIFORM CODE"

LCDR Joseph K. Taussig Jr., USN

Moving from the debate just before the adoption of the Uniform Code of Military Justice (UCMJ) to the reaction of military leaders just after that event, this 1951 article discussed new provisions of military law and how they would work in practice. Suggesting a certain degree of skepticism, the author urged Navy officers to take up the work of adapting the new code "to the actualities of life."

"THE COMMANDING OFFICER AND THE NEW UNIFORM CODE"

By LCDR Joseph K. Taussig Jr., USN, U.S. Naval Institute *Proceedings* (October 1951): 1051–55.

Many changes in the administration of discipline and justice will be apparent to the Naval Service while the new *Uniform Code of Military Justice* and the supplementary *Manual for Courts-Martial, United States, 1951* are progressing through their growing pains. The obvious manifestations of these changes will be stories and rumors of miscarriages of justice, technical loopholes exploited by defense counsel, and a feeling of frustration when someone deserving punishment beats the system.

The *Code* and *Manual*, with their appendices, consist of approximately 250,000 words and replace most of the *Articles for the Government of the Navy* and *Courts and Boards*. The purpose of this article is to aid the Commanding Officers of ships and stations in understanding the disciplinary procedures applicable to them, utilizing as little legal language as possible and avoiding too many of the "special cases" which will form the basis of future Court Martial Orders. [...]

By way of introductory instruction, the new Code was enacted by Congress in May 1950 to become effective *in toto* on May 31, 1951. Offenses committed before May 31, 1951, were to be "pleaded" (that is, the Charge and Specifications written) under the old Courts and Boards, but the procedures of the courts are to follow the new procedures outlined in the *Code* and *Manual*.

Three types of court will exist. The "General Court-Martial," similar to our present "General Court-Martial"; the "Special Court-Martial," similar to our present "Summary Court-Martial"; and the unfortunately named (for the Navy) "Summary Court-Martial," similar to our present "Deck Court." [...]

First the Commanding Officer should require by positive means that every officer read the *Code* and become familiar with the *Manual*. With the reading an accomplished fact, many of the obvious pitfalls will be avoided. Some discussion will naturally follow if every officer has read the publications. Many questions will arise in the minds of each officer, and having the advantage of a common denominator, even the most disinterested will enter into the discussion even if merely to condemn.

Second, the law itself requires that certain sections be publicized to each enlisted man on his enlistment *and* re-enlistment and at least six months thereafter. This replaces the theoretical reading of "*Rocks and Shoals*" on a monthly basis. (See Article 137 of Code.)

The specific steps in the processes of reaching a legal solution of a disciplinary problem arc outlined briefly below. Where the process wanders from the general trail, the discussion will be curtailed.

A typical act, the seriousness of which can spread-eagle the field of punishment, might involve the operation of a vehicle. The offense could range from a mere traffic violation of minor importance through hit-and-run manslaughter.

The actual process of bringing an accused to justice starts by "initiating the charge." Any person, whether subject to the *Code* or not, may do this. The process involved consists of merely bringing to the attention of the proper military authorities the fact that an offense has been committed. In a traffic offense this may be a civilian police report, a report by any person performing military police duties or any other observer.

The next requisite after the initiating of the charge is "apprehension." Although the *Manual* has several sections on apprehension in anticipation of the unusual cases, the basic idea is that all persons (above seaman) and those performing police duties have a duty to apprehend offenders.

Apprehension is defined as the "taking into custody." It is predicted that many CMOs [court-martial orders] will be written on this phase. The person "apprehending" will be allowed to hold the person apprehended, physically, until such time as he can be placed under arrest or confined by a person having that authority, or he may be "apprehended" by merely being informed that he has been apprehended and is in the custody of the apprehender. Consequently, as used, "apprehension" seems to be analogous to the "arrest" performed by the civilian police officer on civilian offenders. Unfortunately, throughout the *Code* and *Manual*, common terms have been used to which a somewhat different technical definition has been assigned by the layman. Thus the first branch in the tree is "apprehension" that is, finding the offender and detaining him morally or physically for further disposition.

Following on the heels of apprehension, three courses of action are open to the command exercising jurisdiction over the person. In the order of severity, the three avenues of further procedure are: restriction, arrest, and confinement. Collectively, they are termed "restraint." Necessary in this step is the determination of who is competent to invoke this restraint.

Basically, the Commanding Officer may impose restraint on any person under his jurisdiction, and he is the only person who can impose such restraint on an officer, warrant officer, or civilian. Any officer can order an enlisted person into arrest or confinement. The Commanding Officer may delegate this authority to a warrant officer or petty officer as he sees fit. The *Manual* provides that any officer authorized to arrest or confine, may within his discretion and without imposing arrest, "restrict" an individual. Thus, the third step the Commanding Officer takes is to delegate that part of his authority to restrain, which the *Manual* allows him to delegate to the extent he sees fit.

The terms "restraint," "arrest," "confinement," and "restriction," as already pointed out, have technical meanings. Thus "restraint" includes the other three terms. "Arrest" as used, is a moral restraint imposed orally or in writing (obviously writing is preferable) and is used to restrict the person's personal liberty while the charges are being disposed of. Under this type of restraint, the person cannot perform his military duties, but may be assigned cleaning and policing duties, and training duties not involving the bearing of arms. Evidently to avoid this inconvenience and save the person for military duties the term "restriction in lieu of arrest" is used, by which the officer authorized to restrain may specify limits similar to arrest, but allow the person to perform his military duties as well.

"Confinement" is a physical restraint, and may be executed on oral or written orders by competent authority. This confinement is to be limited to the time necessary for the disposition of the charges.

All three types of restraint are within the discretion of the restraining officer as he sees fit under the circumstances. The *Manual* provides that, as a matter of policy, confinement should not be used for minor transgressions. Violation of the provisions of the restraint are punishable under the General Article (UCMJ 134).

The accused, once restrained, remains in that condition until released by proper authority (usually the person ordering the arrest or restriction or the commanding officer of the confining activity, as the case may be). For the purposes of clarity, it is pointed out at this stage of the discussion that the technical terms used above are applicable for the stage of proceedings to which they refer. The same terms may be used subsequently for different purposes towards the completion of proceedings. Thus "confinement" may either be awaiting disposition of the charges or pursuant to the sentence of a court.

The next step in the disposition of the offender affords five different solutions: dismissal of the charges, non-judicial punishment or recommendations for summary court-martial, special court-martial, or general court-martial. This step involves judgment. From the facts available, the commander concerned must make a preliminary decision as to which of the four types of punishment will ultimately result or whether the charge can immediately be dismissed. In a vast majority of instances this will not be difficult. A minor traffic violation, for instance, will warrant non-judicial punishment. Hit-and-run manslaughter will warrant a general court-martial. In this decision it is probably better to err on the side of seriousness of offense, but this leads to a more complex routine.

Assuming that the case is a clear-cut non-judicial punishment offense and Captain's Mast will undoubtedly serve justice and discipline, the commander, no matter what the limits of his authority to convene courts-martial are, may bring the offender to mast if he wishes. This procedure has some technicalities.

(1) In the Navy, an accused may not object to non-judicial punishment, as such, and demand a trial as he may in the Army and Air Force.

(2) The accused must be informed as to the nature of the offense.

(3) The accused must be warned that he does not have to make any statement regarding the offense, and that any statement he does make may be used against him as evidence in a trial by court-martial.

(4) The accused has a right to appeal to the next superior in the chain of command if he deems that the punishment is unjust or disproportionate to the offense.

(5) The non-judicial punishment may be pleaded in bar of trial in a court-martial for the same offense for which the punishment is awarded.

At mast, the accuser, if available, should be present and should be given the same warning as the accused as to his right to speak and the use of his statement against him. Similarly, any other witnesses called should be so warned.

The list of punishments which can be awarded are listed in the *Code* and *Manual*. These have been changed considerably from the old standards utilized in the Navy and should be thoroughly studied. If the immediate commander is not morally certain that the offense can be disposed of at mast as a non-judicial punishment, he must then reach a further decision. [...]

As can be seen, there are many deviations imposed on the old system that the Navy followed under the *Articles for the Government of the Navy* and *Courts and Boards*. It will take intelligence and planning to gear the new system to the actualities of life. Whether the individual agrees or disagrees with the new *Code* and *Manual* is entirely immaterial in the augmentation of the new law; it is the law, and fighting it is unmilitary. As time goes on, the more obvious faults will be ironed out by virtue of constructive criticism. Forbearance will be a commendable virtue.

17 "YOU WOULD THINK THEY WERE MORTAL ENEMIES"

(Selection from *The Reminiscences of Lieutenant Commander Richard A. Harralson*)

LCDR Richard A. Harralson, USN (Ret.)

In this oral history interview, a retired Navy officer described his experiences with courts-martial and the new Uniform Code of Military Justice (UCMJ) during his service in the Great Lakes Naval District from 1952 to 1954.

"YOU WOULD THINK THEY WERE MORTAL ENEMIES"

(Selection from *The Reminiscences of Lieutenant Commander Richard A. Harralson, U.S. Navy [Retired]*) by LCDR Richard A. Harralson, USN (Ret.) (Naval Institute Press, 1997) 297–98.

[. . .]

[Interviewer]: Are there any of these court-martial cases that you particularly remember, that were interesting?

Commander Harralson: Most of them were very boring, usually desertion. We had one young man, though. He was a handsome young fellow. And, of course, they come in in nice, clean dress blues and look very upstanding. He was accused of desertion. We found him not guilty of desertion, but guilty of the lesser included offense, of being absent without leave. Then, of course, we entered the sentencing part. The defense stood up and said, "I have matters of mitigation." He told about this young man's poor aunt that lived in Milwaukee, and on and on about that, and got through.

Then the prosecution stood up and said, "I have matters in aggravation." That kid had been in the Navy four years, his enlistment was about up, and I think the Navy got two months of useful work out of him. He had been court-martialed before and been to captain's mast so many times.

[Interviewer]: Unfortunately, there are a few bad apples that come in.

Commander Harralson: Oh, yes. Oh, another thing, though, that impressed me was that the lawyers were Navy lieutenants. They don't call it prosecution; they call them the defense counsel and the trial counsel—two lieutenants. They would go after it, hammer and tongs. You would think they were mortal enemies. They insulted each other. They put on a show. But after one trial, I had a car problem and needed a ride to Forrestal Village. I knew this one lawyer lived over there, this one lieutenant, so I asked him for a ride and he said, "Sure." He said, "I've got another ride, we have to wait for." So we waited there, in the car. Pretty soon, the other lawyer showed up.

[Interviewer]: The one he'd been insulting?

Commander Harralson: Yes. [Laughter] These guys were bosom buddies. They lived next door to each other.

[Interviewer]: They were just doing their jobs. [Laughter]

Commander Harralson: Exactly. No offense.

[Interviewer]: Well, I would expect a lot of these are pretty much cut and dried; the facts are clear-cut and so forth.

Commander Harralson: Yes. Desertion is a little hard to prove, because it involves intent to stay away forever. But there were certain things that could be taken into account, like getting rid of all uniforms, and destroying ID cards, and living under an assumed name. You'd begin to suspect he didn't intend to come back. [Laughter]

18 "CAVEAT: THE MANUAL FOR COURTS-MARTIAL"

Col Hamilton M. Hoyler, USMC

Published a decade after the adoption of the Uniform Code of Military Justice (UCMJ), this article discussed the significant legal effects of another development in military justice: the creation of the Courts of Military Appeals, a first for the U.S. armed forces. The court, now called the Court of Appeals for the Armed Forces, opened in 1951. In practice, the presence of an appeals court for the military justice system provided important due process protections for court-martial defendants.

"CAVEAT: THE MANUAL FOR COURTS-MARTIAL"

By Col Hamilton M. Hoyler, USMC, U.S. Naval Institute *Proceedings* (January 1960): 58–69.

[...]

When the Court of Military Appeals began to sit almost nine years ago, the complaints raised in Congress and elsewhere about the shortcomings of the court-martial system were still in the air. The principal objections were to something called "command control" and to the fact that an accused tried by court-martial lacked certain constitutional rights accorded an accused tried in civilian courts. During the nine years of its existence the Court of Military Appeals has been principally concerned with protecting the accused from command influence and providing him with rights analogous to those of a civilian tried in the criminal courts. In its efforts to safeguard the accused, the Court of Military Appeals has in many instances enlarged the rights of the accused beyond the limits provided in the Manual for Courts-Martial.

Command control is the term used to describe the authority of commanding officers to appoint and control courts-martial. Under the old system the same official could:

Accuse the offender.

Direct what charge would be preferred.

Select the prosecutor, defense counsel and members of the court.

Review the record.

Admonish the court if he disagreed with the result.

It was believed that this much power in the hands of one man would prevent the accused from getting an impartial trial. The record of Congressional debate on the Uniform Code of Military Justice is full of references to commanders and their

"Unfair and arbitrary practices."

"Capricious and whimsical action."

"Overbearing and authoritarian spirit."

"Hardboiled and arrogant methods."

So strong were these objections to command control that it was seriously proposed that court-martial authority be removed from military commanders and given to the civilian courts or to a judge advocate general corps. The majority of the Congress, however, recognized that the trial of a military offender could not be removed from a military commander without destroying discipline. The problem of command control was summed up by Congressman Vinson in the following words: "Our problem stems from our desire to create an enlightened system of military justice which not only preserves and protects the rights of the members of our armed forces, but also recognizes the sole reason for the existence of a military establishment—the winning of wars."

To eliminate command control Congress attempted to draw a line between the commander's duty to enforce military law and his power to influence its administration. The general Congressional intent to remove command control was spelled out in Article 37 of the Uniform Code of Military Justice and the accuser concept. Article 37 provided that no person could coerce or influence a court-martial or any member with respect to his judicial acts. A convening authority was specifically forbidden from punishing anyone connected with judicial proceedings. As stated in the Uniform Code of Military Justice, the accuser concept provides in substance: Anyone who has "an interest other than an official interest" in the prosecution of the accused is an accuser, and an accuser cannot convene a special or general court-martial.

But exactly what did the law mean when it said an accuser was anyone who had an "interest, other than an official interest, in the prosecution of the accused?"

An answer to this question was provided in the case of *U.S. v Gordon*. On 5 March, Gordon, an airman, broke and entered General Edwards' house at Bolling Air Force Base. On 9 March, Gordon burgled General Lee's house. General Lee was the Base Commander at Bolling. On 10 March, Gordon was apprehended and confessed to both offenses. On 27 March, charges were preferred by the provost marshal against Gordon and on 2 April General Lee convened a General Court-Martial. Upon completion of the pre-trial investigation which must precede a General Court-Martial, the Investigating Officer recommended that Gordon be tried by General Court-Martial for breaking into General Edwards' house, but that the charge of breaking into General Lee's house be dropped. The Staff Legal Officer recommended the same thing. General Lee ordered Gordon to be tried for breaking into the Edwards house and the charge of burglary of the Lee house was dropped. Gordon was duly convicted of burglary of General Edwards' quarters. After the trial Gordon appealed on the grounds that General Lee was an accuser and had no power to convene a court in his case.

The question presented to the Court of Military Appeals hinged on this matter of what interest General Lee had in the proceedings. General Lee did not sign the charges nor did he direct that charges be signed. He was, however, a victim of the burglary and he did convene the court-martial which convicted the accused. This, said the accused, made him an accuser. The Court of Military Appeals ruled that General Lee was an accuser. Not only did he know of the offense, but it was reasonable to believe that he had more than official interest in the prosecution of the accused. The Court of Military Appeals said that the accused is entitled to an impartial trial and to an impartial review by an officer free from any connection with the controversy.

But suppose the convening authority was not personally involved with the accused's offense? Suppose the offender is charged with violating an order signed by the convening authority? The Marsh case provides an answer to this question.

After a period of AWOL, Marsh, a soldier, reported into an army post. He was given stragglers orders directing him to report to a port of embarkation. In addition, he was given another piece of paper captioned "Direct Order." This "Direct Order" was signed "By Command of Lt. General Hodges" the commanding general of the post. It directed him to proceed to the port of embarkation and indicated trial by General Court-Martial if he disobeyed. Marsh went UA again and was tried for disobedience of a direct order by a court convened by General Hodges. After conviction, Marsh appealed claiming Lt. General Hodges was the accuser because his direct order had been violated. The Court of Military Appeals agreed with Marsh and said that because a direct order issued by General Hodges has been violated that General Hodges had a personal interest in the matter and was therefore an accuser.

The Gordon and the Marsh cases indicated that as commanders we must insure that our interest in the enforcement of military law is always kept on the official level and that we should never become involved in what could be construed as a personal controversy or a direct relationship with the accused. [. . .]

So much for the accuser concept and the problem of personal interest versus official interest. Let us now look at some examples of interference by the convening authority in court-martial processes. [...]

Examples of interference by a convening authority in court-martial processes have been found most frequently in connection with paragraph 38 MCM. This paragraph provides that a convening authority through the staff legal officer, or otherwise, may give general instruction "to personnel of courts-martial relating to "rules of evidence, burden of proof, and presumption of innocence, and may include information as to the state of discipline in the command . . . and command measures . . . taken to prevent offenses." In both of the cases which follow the accused claimed that the convening authority had improperly influenced the court under the guise of giving instruction.

Three months before the trial of an accused by the name of Navarre, the convening authority assembled all of his officers and gave them two hours' instruction on the Uniform Code of Military Justice. He discussed improper findings and sentences in previous courts-martial and presented statistics which indicated that noncommissioned officers were more often acquitted and given lighter sentences than other enlisted men. He stated that he would make notations on the fitness reports of officers who failed to carry out their duties under the Uniform Code of Military Justice. Three months after this session, Navarre was convicted by a court-martial which included members who had been instructed by the convening authority. Navarre claimed improper command influence.

In the Ferguson case the accused and three others were charged with mutiny in the brig. The day before the trial, the commanding officer, chief of staff, staff legal officer, the law officer and the members of the court were assembled for instruction by the staff legal officer. He stated the general duties of court members and then discussed disciplinary problems at the post. He mentioned "dissident elements" and "trouble makers" and the need for prompt and firm handling of such cases. Ferguson was convicted, and he appealed on the grounds of command influence.

How do the cases compare?

The Court of Military Appeals in the Navarre case said that the commanding officer acted properly to take affirmative action to insure fair trials.

Under the circumstances, the Court of Military Appeals said the reference to fitness reports was not improper. But in the Ferguson case they held that the connection between the staff legal officer's advice and the trial of the accused for mutiny the following day was so direct as to create a bias against the accused.

So far we have dealt with situations where the command influence has been held to be a direct or personal influence exerted by the commanding officer or the convening authority. But the most important application of the doctrine of command influence does not involve the commanding officer or the convening authority at all. This new twist to the doctrine has only recently been announced.

We are all familiar with various Secretary of the Navy and Secretary of the Defense policy instructions regarding discipline in the Naval Establishment. For example, Secretary of the Navy Instruction 5815.2A dated 12 March 1956 states Navy Department policy regarding larceny and other offenses involving moral turpitude. The instruction indicates that a thief should not be retained in the service. Paragraph 33 h of the Manual for Courts-Martial contains a similar policy statement; ". . . that the retention in the armed forces of thieves and persons guilty of moral turpitude injuriously reflects upon the good name of the military service." Do these statements reflect command influence?

In the case of an accused named Estrada the Trial Counsel invited the court's attention to the policy of the Secretary of the Navy regarding larceny and offenses involving moral turpitude. The court said that reading Secretary of the Navy Instruction 5815.2A to the court is the same as calling the Secretary of the Navy to the stand and asking him what instructions he has with regard to the case before the court. This, said the Court of Military Appeals, is the strongest kind of command influence.

In the case of a Coast Guard officer named Rinehart the Trial Counsel directed the court's attention to paragraph 33 h, Manual for Courts-Martial. The Court of Military Appeal held that the introduction of any policy directive, whether in the Manual for Courts-Martial or not, was for the purpose of influencing the court in its deliberations and was improper. Again, the Court of Military Appeals stressed the doctrine of command influence. [. . .]

[. . .] To get the picture of what the Court of Military Appeals has in mind, remember the doctrine of separation of powers in our federal government between the executive, legislative, and judicial branches. It is apparently the Court of Military Appeals' objective to develop military courts which will have the same freedom from executive control that civilian courts enjoy.

To provide the military accused with the same rights enjoyed by a civilian tried in the criminal courts, the Court of Military Appeals has not only spent much time in the explanation and definition of those rights, but has often expanded them beyond the limits set forth in the Manual for Courts-Martial. This process falls under three general headings:

The development of the doctrine of military due process.

The expansion of the rights of the accused beyond the Manual for Courts-Martial.

The expansion of the rights of the accused beyond the Uniform Code of Military Justice.

One of the earliest doctrines announced by the Court of Military Appeals was the doctrine of "military due process." According to the court "Congress intended to place military justice on the same plane as civilian justice." Therefore, said the court, its duty was to give the same legal effect to the rights granted by Congress to military personnel as do the civilian courts to those granted to civilians by the constitution and other federal statutes. The phrase "military due process" is analogous to the phrase "due process of law" found in the Constitution and refers to the minimum standards of military justice which must be met before an accused can be convicted. [. . .]

Through the doctrine of military due process the court has announced its intention to provide liberal protection for the accused throughout the whole field of military law. Under the doctrine of military due process, the accused is protected by a strict interpretation of his rights as stated in the Manual for Courts-Martial and the Uniform Code of Military Justice. In its desire to protect the accused, however, the court has often given him many additional rights which the Manual for Courts-Martial as written does not give him. It is in this area of judge-made extensions to the Manual for Courts-Martial that we must be particularly careful to avoid error. The discussion that follows does not cover all of these judge-made extensions to the Manual for Courts-Martial but only some of the most important.

The first group of cases extending the rights of the accused beyond the Manual for Courts-Martial concern Paragraph 150, Manual for Courts-Martial. This paragraph deals with the privilege against self-incrimination. After explaining the privilege which prohibits a person from being forced to give evidence against himself, the Manual for Courts-Martial makes the following statement: "This prohibition . . . relates only to the use of compulsion in obtaining . . . a verbal or other communication . . . and does not forbid compelling (an accused) to exhibit his body or other physical characteristics. . . ." The paragraph goes on to say it is all right to use force to take a person's fingerprints, to take samples of his handwriting, to make him speak for purposes of voice identification and ends with the statement that "the prohibition is not violated by requiring a person . . . to submit to having . . . a sample of his blood taken." If it is all right to take blood samples, it would seem that urine samples could be properly obtained. Urine samples are often important in drug addiction cases.

In the case of an accused named Williamson, a sample of urine was obtained by catheter and analyzed. The accused was unconscious when the sample was taken. Later at his trial he objected to using the analysis of his urine against him on the grounds that he was compelled to give evidence against himself. The Court of Military Appeals, following the Manual for Courts-Martial, said that there was nothing improper in the procedure.

The court reached a different result a few months later. In the Jones case, urine was also obtained from an accused by catheter. This time the accused was conscious and he objected strenuously. In the case of *U.S. v Jorden* the accused disobeyed an order to provide a sample of urine and was tried for disobedience of orders. In both the Jones and the Jorden cases the Court of Military Appeals said that to require an accused to provide a urine sample was a violation of the privilege against self-incrimination.

Why did the court change its mind? The answer lies in a decision by the U.S. Supreme Court in the case of *Rochin v. California*. In the *Rochin* case the civilian authorities had used a stomach pump on a narcotics suspect to obtain evidence from his stomach. The pump was applied by force against the violent objections of the accused. The Supreme Court said such procedure violated the Fifth Amendment which provides that no person shall be compelled to be a witness against himself.

As an example of another part of the Manual for Courts-Martial changed by the Court of Military Appeals, let us turn to cases dealing with Paragraph 164 of the Manual for Courts-Martial. Paragraph 164 of the Manual for Courts-Martial discusses desertion and includes the following statement: "If the condition of absence without proper authority is much prolonged and there is no satisfactory explanation of it, the court will be justified in inferring from that alone an intent to remain absent permanently."

Since the *Cothern* case was decided, it is prejudicial error for this statement to be read to the court. In the *Cothern* case the accused was charged with desertion for seventeen days' absence. He presented evidence of family difficulties and denied an intention to desert. As part of his instructions, the law officer read the passage from the Manual for Courts-Martial about prolonged absence being enough from which to infer an intent to remain away permanently from the service. The accused was convicted of desertion and the conviction was approved by a Navy Board of Review. On appeal the Court of Military Appeals threw the conviction out. The court said that neither the law officer nor the Manual for Courts-Martial may substitute a period of absence, regardless of its length, for the ingredient of intent. They pointed out that length of absence is merely one fact from which an intent to desert can be inferred. [. . .]

[. . .] Of equal significance to us is the additional protection which the Court of Military Appeals as given the accused which seems to extend beyond the code itself. The first example of this extra protection to the accused concerns the enlargement of the right of the accused to counsel prior to trial.

The Uniform Code of Military Justice provides that an accused is entitled to appointed defense counsel on three occasions: at the pretrial investigation, during the trial, and on appeal. The code specifies that the defense counsel in trials by General Court-Martial must be a lawyer. It specifies that an appellate defense counsel must also be a lawyer. The code does not require that a lawyer must be appointed as counsel at pre-trial investigations. Recently, however, in the case of *U.S. v Tomaszewski* the court ruled that an accused at a pre-trial investigation is entitled to a lawyer as counsel.

But what about a suspect's right to counsel during a preliminary investigation? The *Gunnels* case provides an answer to this question. During a preliminary investigation by the CID, Gunnels, the accused, asked for counsel. The CIC took him to the staff legal office but none of the lawyers would talk to him. The investigation was resumed and Gunnels answered several questions. A few days later, after charges were preferred against Gunnels, the CID reopened the investigation. This time Gunnels was accompanied by a military lawyer. But the lawyer was not permitted to be present during the interrogation. Gunnels was convicted on evidence obtained from him at the preliminary inquiry. On appeal the conviction was reversed.

The Court of Military Appeals said three things were wrong in the *Gunnels* case: (1) A suspect has the right to consult a civilian lawyer of his choice or a staff legal officer even before charges are preferred. (2) He has a right to have a counsel present during preliminary investigation. (3) He must be advised of his right to consult counsel and to have counsel present during interrogation.

Putting these cases together we can state this rule with respect to the right of the accused to counsel prior to trial: At a preliminary investigation, an accused, upon request, is entitled to be represented by military or civilian counsel or to consult a staff legal officer. At a pre-trial investigation, the accused is entitled to appointed military legal counsel or to a civilian lawyer of his choice. [. . .]

[. . .] The task of administering our military law is steadily becoming more and more demanding. As we have seen, we can no longer rely on the Manual for Courts-Martial for guidance to the extent that we could in the past. Nor can we unload our responsibility in this field on the legal officer. The task of shaping our military law rests on all of us. As stated by the court in the Plummer case, it is our responsibility to hasten the day when "all military personnel, legal and non-legal, will realize that they have a joint obligation with civilians to share in the development of military law as an integral part of American Jurisprudence."

19 "PEOPLE MADE AN EFFORT TO BE JUST"

(Selection from *The Reminiscences of Vice Admiral Robert Taylor Scott Keith*)

VADM Robert Taylor Scott Keith, USN (Ret.)

In this oral history interview from the 1980s, a retired Navy officer described the origins of the crisis in naval justice during World War II. Keith commanded a destroyer squadron in 1946 and served in the Philippines from 1957 to 1959. Here again, an officer who served before the Uniform Code of Military Justice was in place defends the old system of naval justice—"I never saw any fairer system than that for trial"—while arguing that fairness in courts-martial is a product of a love of service and a commitment to the profession.

"PEOPLE MADE AN EFFORT TO BE JUST"

(Selection from *The Reminiscences of Vice Admiral Robert Taylor Scott Keith, U.S. Navy [Retired]*) by VADM Robert Taylor Scott Keith, USN (Ret.) (Naval Institute Press, 1987): 121–24.

[...]

I'm very happy that I didn't make the decision to be a lawyer, but I did have a good deal of experience in the Navy's legal line. A lot of it came after we switched over from the old Courts and Boards to the new manuals. Before I went to the *Missouri* [*Editor's note:* in 1954], I was chief of staff to Admiral

[Charles C.] Hartman, Commander Destroyers Atlantic, and he had general court-martial authority for all the New England area. So I read a good many courts every month. I reviewed all the big courts and the summary courts-martial and took them in to him for signature.

Later I went to the Philippines, and there I had general court-martial authority for the Philippines. One interesting thing there was amusing. Because when I was a squadron commander in destroyers, I had had occasion to research old court-martial orders, looking for an authority to disapprove a court that I wanted to get off the record. A sailor man was accused of stealing government whiskey from a radar picket ship that was in my squadron. The Navy authorized captains of radar picket ships transiting the Panama Canal on their way to the picket stations off Okinawa to fortify the government ration of rum to the extent that when they'd had a rough day on the picket line, they could issue a tot of rum to the crew from their own stores. The skippers were allowed to buy it out of bond in Panama at their own expense.

After the war, some of the picket ships hadn't gotten really broken in out there and hadn't been damaged on the picket stations, and the captains had a good deal of liquor left over. One of them tried to recoup, in this particular instance. When his officers were going ashore at some little port somewhere after the war—along the China coast, or the Philippines, or wherever they might be—he would let them buy a bottle of booze. He wouldn't let them drink on board ship, but they could take it ashore with them and have a drink.

Well, he kept this supply locked up in the government liquor locker, and the sailors knew where it was. On Thanksgiving night, they went down, and they took some of the liquor, and they were charged with stealing government property. It was pretty evident it was the captain's property; it wasn't government property. I didn't want all the little young eager lawyers that had come into the Navy during the war to get ahold of this bungling of justice; they'd recommended him for some severe punishment. So I was looking for somebody to disapprove the court and get it off the record. I finally found out from court-martial orders, after two weeks' research back in Saipan, that if the evidence of a co-conspirator was used to convict a man who was pleading not guilty, and if the evidence given by the co-conspirator freely, if he wasn't tried first—the co-conspirator that was giving the evidence—that they couldn't use his evidence against the man who they were going to try to convict under this so-called pal's evidence. So I disapproved the court.

When we got to the Philippines a number of years later, a couple of sailors and a couple of Filipinos stole an LST. They took it outside the bay of Subic, and they took the engine out of it. A few days later, we found the hulk, with no engines in it, drifting somewhere off of Subic. Well, somehow or other, the naval intelligence people got on the trail of these two sailors, and finally they got a confession out of one of them. I had a staff of seven lawyers working for me; the senior one was a captain. He came in one afternoon, bringing two general courts-martial for me to sign, ordering them tried by a general court-martial. I read them over, and I looked up at him, and I said, "Which one of these are you going to try first?"

He said, "Whichever court's ready. It doesn't make any difference."

I said, "I'm not real sure that you are correct legally on this point. Would you check to see whether or not you can use the evidence of a co-conspirator against his co-conspirator, unless he's been tried first."

He looked at me almost in amazement, and he took the courts and went out. He came back two days later and said, "I'll be damned if I know how you did it, but that's right." [Laughter] So that established me as a legal eagle. [. . .]

But we were in a situation then where we'd had the new legal system, I think, foisted upon us, because in World War II, when we established courts-martial ashore to try deserters or AWOL cases, they were mostly manned by recalled retirees. I don't know whether your knowledge goes back to the fact that when we established the selection law in 1934, we had "retained and best fitted" lieutenants in the Navy. A lot of those retained lieutenants were brought back as lieutenant commanders in the war, and a lot of the lieutenant commanders who were under the previous to 1934 system were brought back as lieutenant commanders or commanders in the Navy. A lot of those who had no recent experience in the Navy were assigned to take up these shore billets and let other people go to sea.

The reaction to their arrogance as members of courts-martial, that, "I know this man's guilty, and we're going to hang him," regardless of any evidence to the contrary. The young lawyers just out of law school, that riled the hell out of them. The young lawyers that saw this going on were the ones that got us into trouble under the old Courts and Boards.

I served on lots of courts and boards in the days when we were at sea, and I never saw any fairer system than that for trial. It was certainly as fair as our courts are today in the civilian world. People spent a lot of time. My evidence to you of spending two weeks researching one court-martial—true, I was looking for something in particular, but when court-martial orders came out, I read them all. When I was an ensign, on a summary court-martial, I was alert to what had happened and the decision made in court-martial. You could turn to the index and find in the old court-martial orders similar cases to the one that you had before you. People made an effort to be just, be fair, and to provide assistance to the sailor that was in trouble. I've defended many of them.

The mistake was in using people who were doing their duty, but really not with any great love of the service that they were serving. That love of your service has got to be an influence on your actions. You don't do anything that's going to really hurt, if you can avoid it, if you love it.

20 "DISCIPLINE IN THE NAVAL RESERVE"

CDR R. E. Slivers, USNR

In this 1966 essay, a Navy Reserve commander discussed the unique problem of military justice for reservists—which involves, among other things, the practical question of when a reservist becomes subject to the Uniform Code of Military Justice.

"DISCIPLINE IN THE NAVAL RESERVE"

By CDR R. E. Slivers, USNR, U.S. Naval Institute *Proceedings* (April 1966): 104–11.

[. . .]

The Regular Navy has a host of punishments by which to enforce its will through a variety of courts, both judicial and nonjudicial processes. The threat of court-martial and the punishments that can ensue therefrom, and even so elementary a thing as deprivation of liberty, are powerful levers for the enforcement of discipline. For all practical purposes, these levers are not available to command in the Naval Reserve, even though the Uniform Code of Military Justice (UCMJ) quite obviously stands over both components of the Naval Establishment. There has been only a handful of courts-martial proceedings originating in misconduct by reservists while on inactive duty training, and these prosecutions have ended in few convictions.

It is true that the reservist has sworn to obey the lawful orders of officers appointed over him, and that those so appointed have sufficient authority to enforce discipline, but the circumstances of the inactive duty drill are such that neither the oath nor the authority can be meaningfully brought into play as a means of implementing punitive discipline. In counterbalance, however, it is interesting to observe that flagrant violations of discipline rarely occur during the inactive duty drill, perhaps because the reservist's commitment is so tenuous that it is easier for him to walk away from it than to face the disagreeable results of prospective disciplinary action. Certainly, it requires but little patience for him to defer a violation of military law until he has come under the more lenient civil law.

It is appropriate, therefore, to examine some of the violations of discipline which *are* committed by reservists during inactive duty training. Since the Court of Military Appeals has prescribed narrowly the circumstances in which a reservist is presumed to have entered upon naval duty, these violations are for the most part limited to those offenses defined in the UCMJ under Article 89 (disrespect); Articles 90, 91, and 92 (disobedience); Article 115 (malingering); Article 108 (loss, damage, destruction or wrongful disposition of military property of the United States); and, finally Article 121 (larceny and wrongful appropriation).

Disrespect has no counterpart among civilian felonies or misdemeanors. It is purely a military offense, because mutual respect is peculiarly essential to the discipline of a military organization. It is based on the customs of the service, more or less as unwritten law. Disrespect usually involves vile or obscene language, but it can also involve mute actions such as deliberately walking away from a superior while being spoken to, or by making certain gestures when a superior's back is turned. Disrespect is a violation of discipline which must always be quickly noted and immediately acted upon, because like an infectious and endemic disease it can spread rapidly among men in a military organization by destroying regard for authority. This is not to say, however, that respect for authority can ever be created and maintained by punitive discipline alone; it must always be earned. The effect of an individual case of disrespect is proportional to the strength of overriding respect held by other members of the unit.

Disobedience of a lawful command or directive is not uncommon in the Naval Reserve, but its manifestations are ordinarily subtle and delayed. Direct and immediate disobedience is exceptionally uncommon, and it seldom occurs that commands issued by a superior officer are presumed not to be lawful. Here again, however, the three hours, once a week—or two days, once a month—exposure to military discipline experienced by the inactive duty reservist presents an extraordinary problem. The time lapse between drills provides the reservist with a convenient opportunity to fail to remember an order, and to devise a number of excuses based on the intervening civilian life which the commanding officer cannot easily disprove and which he must accept at face value. Just as in the Regular Navy, the gravity of the offense of disobedience is not found so much in the act of refusing a lawful command but rather that it represents defiance of authority. The question of intent is paramount. The principal deficiency in Naval Reserve discipline is an unconscious tendency to place a personal interpretation upon compliance with an order, and this usually arises more from the heart than the head, more from a lack of knowledge and training than from intent, and from uncertainty as to the meaning and sincerity of the order. It therefore behooves every commanding officer to be sure that all orders and directives are so plainly and emphatically delivered that ignorance of their existence and purpose cannot be a defense by any offender.

Of all the results in discipline to be sought in training, obedience is the most important because it is the psychological pathway to desired habitual reaction.

Malingering is based upon laziness and an unwillingness to perform, and it is normally accompanied by a vague complaint of physical disability which cannot be medically substantiated. The nonexistent backache and headache were not first invented in World War II. As a matter of historical record, some of the most ancient laws governing military organizations dealt with the conundrum presented by the individual soldier or sailor who manufactured excuses not to work. Malingering is an escape mechanism practiced by the few to the considerable disadvantage of those whose complaints are genuine. The reservist who departs early from a drill on the rationale of a fabricated pain, not infrequently after being credited with attendance for pay purposes, may well cause others to attempt the same ruse, and he certainly tears the cloth of unit morale. For this reason, malingering is a thorny disciplinary problem. Fortunately, it is not prevalent in the Naval Reserve.

A far more frequently encountered cousin to malingering is the matter of simple "goofing off." This is more a lack of performance than a violation of discipline; but it should be curtailed because eventually it will contribute to the breakdown of discipline.

Absenteeism on the part of the inactive duty reservist is *not* an offense which results in punitive disciplinary action as does *absent without leave* in the Regular Navy. The Naval Reservist participates voluntarily, and can in the same sense decide not to participate. He is completely free to discontinue his affiliation with a unit permanently without prior notice, or to absent himself from any drill or series of drills. He does not by the former remove himself from the Naval Reserve if he has a continuing legal obligation to serve; he merely places himself in another category that is well defined by law. While not lessening any otherwise legal liability for mobilization, he does impose upon himself deprivation of pay and he may jeopardize his opportunity for promotion or advancement. There is a provision of Federal law which permits the Navy to recall or assign to 45 days active duty involuntarily any member of the Ready Reserve who fails satisfactorily to perform inactive duty training, but the Navy so sincerely desires to maintain the Naval Reserve as an organization comprised wholly of volunteers that this type of disciplinary action is not extensively used. It is sometimes applied to pre-active duty personnel below the rank of petty officer, providing such orders to 45 days active duty (or immediate assignment to two years of active duty under the 2x6 program) do not remove the young sailor from high school.

Loss, damage, destruction or wrongful disposition of government property occur as a result of carelessness, and they happen as often as carelessness itself affects a situation where government property is involved. These are not disciplinary matters unless they are intentional rather than negligent. When a reservist in a sudden fit of temper kicks a hole in a Training Center bulkhead or smashes expensive equipment, he is perhaps also guilty of disrespect. Psychiatric examination might be indicated but would be highly impractical. The unit commanding officer would do well to consider an administrative discharge, but at the same time it would be appropriate to examine closely the events which produced such a loss of self-control.

Larceny, like carelessness, is always with us. The case of the purloined wallet is constantly a military aggravation, but then it is similarly a concern in a camp for pre-teenage girls. In general, where reasonable investigation does not reveal the culprit, it is wiser for the unit commanding officer not to institute a search for the "strawberries" in the fashion of the notorious Captain Queeg. A culprit discovered is better turned over to civil authorities! In either case, reinstruction for all hands in the security of personal property is in order.

This brings us to the need to understand when a reservist is subject to the UCMJ. When a reservist enters upon active duty or active duty for training he is inescapably subject to the Navy's standard methods of enforcing discipline. The law specifies that all other times he is subject to the provisions of the UCMJ only while he is (1) actually engaged on inactive duty training which has been (2) authorized by written orders which (3) state that he is subject to the UCMJ, *and only* when those orders are (4) voluntarily accepted by the reservists.

Actually engaged on inactive duty training does not include portal-to-portal transportation from his home to the place of drill or return therefrom. For all practical purposes, his liability to military justice commences when he has physically entered an authorized place of drill at the time of a scheduled drill and has become involved in some phase of an authorized training program, and it ceases when the unit is dismissed by the commanding officer or his designated representative. Not all reservists receive written orders to inactive duty training, but orders normally are written for those who train in one way or another with a pay or nonpay unit, or on appropriate duty. These orders usually provide for an endorsement denoting voluntary acceptance of the provisions of military justice; but whether or not the reservist endorses his orders to this effect, his act of engaging in the duty firmly implies such understanding and voluntary acceptance. Thus, the reservist on inactive duty training is under the disciplinary code of the armed forces only during the three hours of an evening drill or during carefully delineated periods of time during a weekend drill. At all other times, he is liable for his actions under civil law.

Even while he is subject to the UCMJ, the reservist is relatively free from any of the punishments specified in Article 15. It is extremely difficult for a unit commanding officer to submit a reservist to Summary Court Martial during a three-hour drill and his legal detention beyond that time is nearly impossible. The situation is not at all comparable to that which obtains in the Regular Navy whereby a reservist on active duty for training can merely not be released until the effect of arraignment for court martial has materialized. While a reserve unit commanding officer may have the lawful power to hold mast during an inactive duty drill, or to institute court martial proceedings, he is logically prevented from deciding to do so by the realization that such an action may well commit himself, his subordinate officers, and dozens of others to months of complex legal involvement. Administrative mast is not uncommon, but it amounts to little more than a "bawling out," and should this be improperly handled the resulting resentment can lose the Naval Reserve another volunteer.

It is obvious, therefore, that the unit commanding officer must rely upon methods of training and discipline which do not call for the punitive measures set forth in the UCMJ. This is a fact of life in spite of that part of the U.S. Code which says that all laws applying to both regulars and reservists shall be administered without discrimination, and in spite of the fact that the commanding officer of a Naval Reserve unit is unequivocally charged by Navy Regulations with responsibility for the maintenance of discipline among the members of his unit on the basis of the UCMJ. In effect, discipline in the Naval Reserve is the art of the possible.

Regarding as *negative discipline* all forms of punitive enforcement and as *positive discipline* all forms of leadership, some of the resources available to the unit commanding officer can be examined briefly.

Negative discipline in the Naval Reserve is extremely limited, but not injuriously so. Usually the maximum punishment, if such it be, is the administrative discharge for unsuitability, unfitness, or misconduct. This has both advantages and disadvantages. It performs the function of continuous screening required by law to ensure the constant availability of the number of competent Ready Reservists judged by the Congress to be necessary for national defense, and it serves to eliminate trouble makers. At the same time, it complicates a perennially difficult recruiting situation and often takes so long to process that the effect of example is lost to other members of the unit.

Of even longer-range effect but perhaps least desired by Naval Reserve personnel is an unfavorable entry in the service record or damning with faint praise in a fitness report. Here, though, more often than not, the commanding officer is likely to place himself between a rock and a shoal, because in the Naval Reserve far more than in the Regular Navy such an observation is somehow a reflection upon his own leadership.

Keeping in mind that the best discipline is immediate discipline, some unit commanding officers use the time-tested device of disapprobation—in some fashion publishing the names of those guilty of minor infractions such as uniform discrepancies, tardiness, failure to pass examinations or to perform a duty correctly. This procedure often does not approach the severity of negative discipline demanded by more serious offenses, and if carried too far, flies in the face of the axiom: *praise in public, condemn in private.*

All in all, the reserve unit commanding officer is left with positive discipline, and the keynote of all his disciplinary actions must be flexibility.

21 "JUSTICE IN THE BATTLE ZONE"

LCDR James E. Toms, USN

Judge Advocates serving in Vietnam had to be prepared to deliver justice under fire. In this war zone account, first published in 1969, a Navy lawyer describes his experiences in Danang. Of lasting interest in this article is the problem of investigating, charging, and trying American military personnel for war crimes when many of the witnesses are local natives, difficult to find and difficult to question. In one case that overlapped with the Tet Offensive, the author tried to determine "that the witnesses were alive."

"JUSTICE IN THE BATTLE ZONE"

By LCDR James E. Toms, USN, U.S. Naval Institute *Proceedings* (June 1969): 52–57.

[. . .]

The half-dozen of us who comprised the Staff Legal Office, Commander, U.S. Naval Support Activity, Danang (ComNavSuppActDanang), from June 1967 to May 1968 saw first-hand the advantages—not to mention the inconveniences and hazards—of administering wartime military justice by The Book.

It is, indeed, a versatile volume. Abiding as much as possible to both the spirit and the letter of its pages, the legal-beagles of ComNavSuppAct anticipated at least one refinement in the law itself.

An example of anticipating developments in the law involved punitive discharges handed out at special courts-martial. Congress passed legislation requiring the accused in such cases always to be represented by a counsel qualified in the sense of Article 27b UCMJ. When thereafter ComNavSuppAct looked over the cases he had reviewed as Supervisory Authority over the preceding year, only one such accused had not been represented by a lawyer.

To grasp the magnitude of this accomplishment, one has to look at the limited legal manpower and the geographic distribution of the ComNavSuppAct commands for which legal support had to be provided.

Aside from its thousands of personnel in the Danang area, NavSuppAct, has detachments at Tan My, Hue, Dong Ha, Phu Bai, Cua Viet and Chu Lai. Commanding Officer, Enlisted Personnel, Danang, has special court martial convening authority over the men of all detachments except Chu Lai, where Commanding Officer, Enlisted Personnel, Chu Lai, has that authority. In the cases of several detachments, the officers in charge have nonjudicial punishment authority limited by UCMJ, Article 15(b)H. During our tenure in Vietnam, the number of Construction Battalions (SeaBees) in I Corps had grown from eight to 12, and the original brigade headquarters had been supplemented by one additional brigade headquarters and a regimental headquarters. These units were dispersed generally to the same locations as the NavSuppAct detachments. There was also the SeaBee Maintenance Unit, which looked after advance air strips, such as at Khe Sanh, directly subordinate to the NavSuppAct. ComNavSuppAct was the General Court-Martial Convening Authority for all of these units. In addition, ships at sea looked with increasing frequency to the staff legal officer at NavSuppAct Headquarters for assistance and for counsel qualified in the sense of UCMJ, Article 27b.

Throughout the period in question, the average number of lawyers in the Staff Legal Office NavSuppAct was six: a Commander, a lieutenant commander, and four lieutenants. Aside from counsel work in courts-martial, these officers were absorbed in the usual pursuits of an overseas staff legal office, including the legal assistance program, administration and review of foreign claims, staff advice to command, review of pretrial investigations and courts-martial, participation in administrative discharge proceedings, and exercise of a special authority to adjudicate personal claims in the amount of $1,000 or less. (This latter was no small task, $80,000 cash having been disbursed under this authority during the period under discussion.) Luckily, however, time to accomplish all assigned tasks had been provided by a routine that called for a 12-hour day, seven days each week. [. . .]

New arrivals in the staff legal office viewed their surroundings and the "old hands" with mixed emotions. It seemed incongruous to them to see a young judge advocate preparing for a field trip by packing his briefcase, donning his flak jacket and steel helmet, strapping on a cartridge belt from which a full canteen was suspended and draping an M-16 over his shoulder. The image presented by this young stalwart peering out from under his helmet through his Navy issue spectacles might have been amusing but for the sound of distant gunfire. Not surprisingly, new arrivals quickly adopted the same sartorial style for their field trips.

Getting there was indeed, half the battle for the judge advocates, but, on occasion, the very mobility of some of the other naval personnel proved a problem. For instance, there was a case of homicide in which it was suspected that a member or members of one of the coastwise utility boats might be involved. (A thorough investigation resulted in no servicemen being prosecuted for the homicide.) A special agent from the Naval Investigative Service Office and a judge advocate had been quickly dispatched to the scene, but before they arrived the boat had departed in the course of her vital mission of carrying supplies. Since no specific suspect had been identified, the entire crew had departed. The pattern for the investigation was set by the circumstances. Crew members of the boat were interviewed at one terminal or another while the boat carried out her assigned tasks, keeping the supplies moving.

Inevitably, on foreign soil, incidents arise involving American servicemen and the local populace. Vietnam is no exception, and our judge advocates found the language barrier kept them tethered to their translators. Vietnamese is a language rife with stumbling blocks for the foreigner. It is a tonal language containing almost no polysyllabic words. A single arrangement of two, three, or four letters will have as many as six or more totally unrelated meanings depending upon the inflection. It sometimes seems that some of the inflections are beyond the capability of the American tongue to pronounce or the American ear to distinguish. Nor has the language been long in the American catalogue of studies. Finally, none of the Vietnamese-speaking Americans available to the Navy judge advocates possessed the particular talents needed by a courtroom interpreter; and most of the Vietnamese available for translator duty, of course, were even less likely to be familiar with legalese. The judge advocates, then, grew accustomed to listening to a Vietnamese witness chatter excitedly for five minutes, only to have the Vietnamese interpreter translate: "She say she don't know."

The judge advocates set about searching out interpreters who could provide the needed services. Two Navy enlisted men who had studied at the language school were very helpful. After a time Dame Fortune really proved to be a lady—a young Vietnamese lady—who had graduated from law school at the University of Saigon. She had studied American jurisprudence under the tutelage of judge advocates from the Staff of USMACV and was apprenticed in the practice of law in Danang. She had a good command of English and her professional training gave her an insight which she put to use in translating judge advocates' questions into the most appropriate Vietnamese phrases. More than that, she and her employer became good friends of the judge advocates and provided a window of sorts on the local populace, a window otherwise somewhat fogged over by the fact there was no liberty authorized for members of the U.S. Armed Forces in Danang.

Translation was not the only problem presented by the fact that Vietnamese witnesses were frequently required for trials or trial preparation. Locating a known witness often was a major task. Indeed, finding him twice in the same location sometimes proved impossible. The Vietnamese are somewhat less than eager to participate in judicial proceedings, preferring to let matters ride if accommodation cannot be accomplished without official intervention. There-fore, unless the witnesses were in the employ of the U.S. forces, they attempted to avoid being found in some cases. At other times the war disrupted people's routines so that delays in finding them were inevitable.

Sometimes incidents occurred in remote areas, and the accused serviceman was the only English-speaking person involved. On one occasion, a SeaBee working with a small detachment constructing a hospital for the local com-munity was accused of raping a Vietnamese woman. The only witnesses to the events surrounding this accusation were Vietnamese. The language barrier, as usual, was overcome by employment of translators, but the location was acces-sible only by helicopter. Co-ordination was established with the local contin-gent of the National Police, and the witnesses were gathered and interviewed in the preparation for a pretrial investigation.

On the day the pretrial investigating officer scheduled to conduct his hear-ing, however, air transportation suddenly became unavailable because the chop-pers were employed in the more pressing requirement of counteracting the Tet offensive. In that offensive the locale of the intended investigation was tem-porarily overrun by the Viet Cong. Although telephonic communication was maintained with the Americans there, it was some time before it could be deter-mined that the witnesses were alive and available; thereafter the investigation was continued to its proper conclusion.

Frequently, having located Vietnamese witnesses and interviewed them, and even having recorded their testimony in a pretrial investigation pursuant to UCMJ, Article 32, there still remains the problem of getting the witness to the court-martial. Normally, when ground transportation was appropriate, this presented no particular difficulty. But when it became necessary to persuade a Vietnamese peasant in some remote locale to board a helicopter or airplane, it was an entirely different matter. To convince the individual that he was not being torn forevermore from his paddy, the only world he knew, was some-times a herculean task. Yet, somehow, like the Canadian Mounties, the judge advocates always managed to bring in the witnesses.

If getting there was half the battle, the other half was sometimes the bat-tle itself. For example, one day a Chinook seemed to be taking an inordinate amount of time in getting a trial team to one of the outlying commands. When the chopper finally set down, the load-master shouted, "Make it! This place has been under rocket attack!" As soon as the chopper was clear of passengers, it took off. The muddy landscape had an eerie aspect. The tiny plywood shack which served as a passenger terminal had none of the usual groups of Marines loitering about it awaiting transportation. The usually bustling traffic on the perimeter road was nonexistent. Upon closer approach, the trenches revealed men in flak jackets and steel helmets just beginning to get restless in their cramped sanctuaries.

Since no rockets were incoming at the moment, an effort was made to contact the unit that was convening the court-martial and arrange transportation for the trip of three or four miles. There was no waiting in line to get to the telephone, and—will wonders never cease?—it worked. It wasn't long before an intrepid yeoman/driver appeared with a truck to pick up the trial team and deliver the members to the task at hand.

During the course of the trial, in which a man was charged with breaking and entering an exchange store and stealing merchandise, proceedings were interrupted several times by incoming rockets which drove court members and witnesses to cover. One such interruption seemed noteworthy to the defense counsel in his representation of the accused. One of the issues involved in the case was the amount of merchandise stolen. Little of it has been recovered. The defense had raised the possibility that some of the items of merchandise charged against the accused may have disappeared from the store's inventory in a manner not chargeable to the accused. The store manager, testifying in response to defense cross-examination, had just stated that the store was never left unlocked and unattended. Suddenly, the unmistakable whine of "incoming" was heard. Without standing on ceremony, the courtroom was cleared as those in attendance sought cover in nearby bunkers. When the court again came to order, the defense counsel asked the witness.

"Have you been operating the Exchange Store on occasion when there have been rocket attacks such as this?"

"Yes, sir."

"On those occasions have you left the store building to seek shelter in much the same way as we left the courtroom a few minutes ago, or did you stop to take inventory and lock the door on the way out?"

The point was made.

While by no means were all trials and pretrial investigations conducted in the outlying areas subjected to hostile fire, the occurrence described above was not an isolated instance, and the war in Vietnam was not remote to the Navy judge advocates in I Corps.

In spite of the unusual conditions encountered, the Navy is making UCMJ a real instrument of discipline in Vietnam. Both the accused and the government are being properly represented. During the period under discussion, the judge advocates participated in an average of six special courts-martial per week, and in addition, participated in an average of five general courts-martial per month. No prosecution was stymied for lack of speedy trial. Each accused had his day in court as was his due; UCMJ met the challenge of the battle zone.

On the wall in the Staff Legal Office hangs a homely, handpainted cardboard plaque depicting Lady Justice in flowing robes carrying in one hand the traditional scales, in the other hand a Thompson submachine gun. The judge advocates working there are rightly proud to be carrying out the motto on the border of that plaque: "Justice even in War."

22 "I'M NOT IN BUSINESS TO WIN THE CASE"

(Selection from *The Reminiscences of Vice Admiral George P. Steele II*)

VADM George P. Steele II, USN (Ret.)

Judge Advocates and commanders can take different views of the same court-martial, as lawyers worry about winning their case and commanders are obliged to consider larger questions of good military order. In this oral history interview, conducted in 1986, a retired flag officer discusses just such a conflict of views that took place in the early 1970s. This interview is also a good illustration of the opinion that the adoption of the Uniform Code of Military Justice (UCMJ) and the growth of a professional Judge Advocate Corps represented a damaging "civilianization" of military justice.

"I'M NOT IN BUSINESS TO WIN THE CASE"

(Selection from *The Reminiscences of Vice Admiral George P. Steele II, U.S. Navy [Retired])* by VADM George P. Steele II, USN (Ret.) (Naval Institute Press, 1986–87): 415–18.

[. . .] While we're talking about discipline, I must mention the case of the minesweeper that burned and sank. Before I arrived in the fleet, a minesweeper en route from Subic to Guam had gotten about two-thirds of the way, had a fire on board, and sank. The crew had abandoned ship, they'd all been picked up, and nobody was really hurt. Jim Holloway, the fleet commander, convened a court of inquiry into the loss of the ship, and the court of inquiry's report now came to me.

After looking at this, I gave the captain a general court-martial, and several of the other officers and a couple of senior petty officers on the ship lower grade court-martials. The staff judge advocate, a commander, was very good, and I figured that the case would go its own way and turned my attention elsewhere.

But presently we began to have trouble with it. We couldn't constitute a court on Guam that wasn't composed of dentists, supply people or the failed officers so often banished to outposts like Guam—officers who had been passed over three or four times as lieutenant commanders. The staff officers were no doubt very fine in their specialties, but they had no real idea of the legal responsibilities of the captain of a ship, or about the drills that are supposed to be conducted on board, or about the performance of people in emergencies, or other line matters.

Of course, as convening authority, my teeth had been drawn by the legal community many years before in the civilianization of military justice. I couldn't affect this at all. I just saw an unlikely, motley crew being appointed to the courts and wondered what was going to happen.

One of the main reasons for the courts was that the ship had never had any drills, let alone any fire drills for most of a year. The positioning of certain valves was not in accordance with approved and required procedure. They never tested out the foam system. It was just an absolute horror story of maladministration and failure to prepare themselves for a casualty. But once something happened, the captain did get the right report off promptly, he did abandon ship in due form, and he did save his people.

I watched this court being formed in disgust, figuring, "Well, there's nothing I can do about that." We got a message in from the judge advocate handling the prosecution in Guam, a junior lieutenant JAG Corps officer who wanted to come to Yokosuka, where the flagship was at that particular moment, and see me. I called in my judge advocate and asked, "What do you think about this? Would this meeting prejudice my ability to act on the case in any way?"

He said, "No, you ought to see him."

So he came in and said, in short, "Admiral, I'd like to prefer some additional charges." He recommended charging the commanding officer and chief engineer for doing the wrong things once the fire started. He's been talking to the mine force staff people and other commanding officers of minesweepers and figured out that if the captain, in the first five or six minutes, had done two or three things, or if the chief engineer had, the ship could have been saved. It was true that with a properly drilled crew the ship probably could have been saved. Well, I asked the young lawyer, "Why should I do this?"

He said, "If you don't, you're going to lose the case."

I said, "We don't really understand each other. It's not a question of winning or losing the case, in my opinion; it's a question of doing justice. I'm not in business to win the case. I would have liked to have had a fair-minded court, a court experienced enough to handle this, and then see it give an acquittal if the accused is innocent or find him guilty if he is. I don't think the court you have is that experienced, but maybe nonetheless, justice will be done. I am not going to charge these officers for actions in a period of emergency, in the last 30 minutes of the life of the ship. The reason for the sad 30 minutes is because of complete, total abandonment of all naval practice up to that point. In the last few minutes of chaos, a guy is reacting in an emergency, and if he misses a couple of strokes, I don't think it's criminal. I don't think that's punishable. The captain did save his people."

Well, he went away wagging his head, and sure enough, we "lost" the case, if you want to use his premise. The reason that the government failed to get a conviction was that testimony convincing to the courts was presented to the effect that nobody had these drills. An officer from a carrier said, "We never had any such drills." And a destroyer officer came in and said, "We didn't have any such drills." Don't you think I didn't make hay with that with the type commanders, but that's what shot the thing down.

The commanding officer's trial was first, and he was acquitted. Then the executive officer was acquitted. At that point, I threw out all the rest of the cases except a special court-martial of a cowardly chief petty officer who abandoned his charge of the damage control party and cowered in the stern. I figured if the captain couldn't be convicted, I didn't want to see the chief engineer slain for something I really figured was the captain's first responsibility. The chief engineer actually behaved with some heroism during the last 30 minutes, and once I dismissed his court-martial, on one of my trips to Guam, I gave him a medal.

23 "THE CRUEL BUSINESS OF ACCOUNTABILITY"

CAPT John E. Greenbacker, USN (Ret.)

In a piece that bookends the interview with Admiral Steele, this 1977 article examines the "demise of the court-martial as an appropriate vehicle for the disposition of purely professional dereliction," a change the author assigns to the UCMJ. Among topics more recent to the author, the article examines one of the most remarkable peacetime disasters in the U.S. Navy, the 1923 grounding of seven destroyers—with the loss of twenty-three lives—off the coast of Santa Barbara.

"THE CRUEL BUSINESS OF ACCOUNTABILITY"

By CAPT John E. Greenbacker, USN (Ret.), U.S. Naval Institute *Proceedings* (August 1977): 24–30.

[…]

The most publicized recent instance of a collision between a maneuvering aircraft carrier and her plane guard ship occurred the evening of 22 November 1975 when the USS *Belknap* (CG-26) collided with the flight deck overhang of the USS *John F. Kennedy* (CV-67). Eight crew members died, and 48 others were injured. In this case general courts-martial did follow for the captain and the officer of the deck of the *Belknap*, but with what many considered to be bizarre results. Neither appeared before a general court-martial made up of his professional peers. Each, in accordance with his legal right, was tried before a military judge only. In the case of the commanding officer, who was watching a movie in the *Belknap*'s wardroom until the final, inevitable moments before the collision, the issue was narrowed to the question of whether he had left the ship in the hands of a properly qualified set of watchstanders. He was found not guilty on the determination by the military judge that the prosecution had not even established a *prima facie* case. The officer of the deck was found guilty, but no punishment was assigned on the military judge's determination that the very conviction by a general court-martial was by itself an adequate and appropriate punishment.

These amazing judicial resolutions naturally created a considerable amount of heartburn among many old and not-so-old sea dogs. One can fairly conjecture that the Navy will not again, in like circumstances, attempt to use the court-martial as a vehicle for enforcing the professional accountability of those in charge of its ships at sea.

The demise of the court-martial as an appropriate vehicle for the disposition of purely professional dereliction—in other than the rarest of cases involving willfulness or recklessness—might have been foreseen in 1951 with the substitution of the Uniform Code of Military Justice (UCMJ) for the venerable Articles for the Government of the Navy. Following World War II, public concern over alleged abuses of disciplinary authority, undue command influence over the outcome of courts-martial, and inconsistencies of treatment among the services led to the enactment of the UCMJ and its greatly increased protection of the rights of an accused. The previous code was designed to ensure the maintenance of discipline and standards of performance and to prevent and punish purely criminal acts. The new UCMJ gave major emphasis to the criminal acts. Subsequent enactments and judicial interpretations intensified this characteristic to such an extent that there is today little difference between a prosecution by court-martial and trial in a federal district court. Over the years, the law officer of a general court martial has gradually assumed greater and greater control over the proceedings. By now, the function of the members of a general court-martial is essentially that of a jury. Furthermore, a court-martial defendant enjoys a right greater than that provided by federal district courts. He is entitled to the right of trial by military judge alone, unfettered by the limitation in the federal courts of prosecution concurrence. It is significant that this right was also exercised by the commanding officer of the USS *Frank E. Evans* (DD-754) after that ship's 1969 collision with the Australian aircraft carrier *Melbourne*. He was found guilty and sentenced to a reprimand on charges of negligence and dereliction of duty. While the long-range wisdom of choosing a one-man court may be questionable from a career viewpoint, it is obviously considered by defendants in such cases to offer an advantage at trial.

The practical result of all this is that, except in cases of criminal negligence or willful misconduct, courts-martial will no longer effectively deal with errors in the judgment of well-intentioned men responsible for the safety of the Navy's ships and their crews. This was illustrated in the trial of the *Belknap*'s captain. The alleged violation of a Navy regulation making the commanding officer responsible for the safety and efficiency of his command was dismissed by the military judge on the basis that the regulation in question constituted a guideline for performance only and could not be enforced by criminal sanctions.

Supporting this approach is the concept of criminal intent. Such intent must be present under our system of criminal justice, in actuality or by presumption, before a finding of guilty may be reached. In the case of criminal negligence, the degree of negligence is such as to be deemed to provide the requisite criminal intent. This contrasts with that level of negligence for which redress is normally had by the aggrieved party through civil action. The distinction may be slight in many cases, but it is nevertheless important in the current applications of the Uniform Code of Military Justice.

It has not always been so. In perhaps the Navy's most spectacular peacetime disaster, a squadron commander led seven of his fourteen destroyers onto the rocks near Point Arguello, California, on 8 September 1923. He was found guilty of "culpable inefficiency in the performance of duty" and of "negligently permitting vessels of the Navy to run upon rocks or shoals." The first charge related only to standards of professional performance, containing the protective word "culpable" to convey the requirement for a serious level of inefficiency before court-martial charges could be found proved. Gone from the Uniform Code of Military Justice is this offense, together with the more colorful language of the Articles for the Government of the Navy, such as "rocks or shoals."

There were other courts-martial associated with the Point Arguello disaster, and two of them illustrate a feature of the old system which is absent from the new. This is the concept of exoneration, an essential tool in any set of procedures for the regulation of professional conduct and the maintenance of standards of professional performance. Of the 11 officers tried for the loss of the seven destroyers, two division commanders and six of the commanding officers were found not guilty. There was, however, a significant distinction in the acquittal of charges. The six commanding officers were simply "acquitted." The two division commanders were "fully and honorably acquitted." The meaning of this distinction was that while the charges against the commanding officers were not proved beyond a reasonable doubt, those against the division commanders not only were not proved beyond a reasonable doubt but their actions with respect to the charges were found by the court to be blameless. This was exoneration of these two officers. Criminal codes in this country, including the Uniform Code of Military Justice, do not provide for exoneration. Other than dismissal of charges for technical legal reasons, acquittal comes only because guilt cannot be established beyond a reasonable doubt. Nothing more can be inferred from such an acquittal. Even a preponderance of the evidence, sufficient for liability in civil cases, does not meet the more rigorous standard of proof in criminal cases. The innocent accused, civilian or military, may well be deserving of exoneration, but neither the federal and state criminal codes nor the Uniform Code of Military Justice can give it to him.

All eight not guilty findings in the Point Arguello cases were disapproved by the Secretary of the Navy on the recommendation of the Judge Advocate General. This was a meaningless disagreement with the results. But it is significant that although Washington did not like the verdicts, the eight were found not guilty by a panel of their professional peers, two of them fully exonerated. The subsequent careers of these officers bore out the judgment of the general court-martial. Exoneration could then, of course, and can now come in other ways. An investigation or court of inquiry can recommend exoneration, but it can recommend only. If the convening authority does not agree, he can still take disciplinary action or institute judicial proceedings. The court-martial under the Articles for the Government of the Navy could exonerate with finality.

The expression of departmental disapproval in the Point Arguello cases was not unusual in such cases and perhaps reflects too narrow a range of sanctions available to courts-martial, even under the old Articles for the Government of the Navy. When the courts-martial which resulted from the 1950 grounding of the USS *Missouri* (BB-63) were in process, the convening authority, searching the precedents, examined every major grounding case which had occurred in the Navy over the preceding 30 years. In almost all such cases, the punishments imposed were viewed by the Navy Department as inadequate, although none of these endorsements offered any guidance as to what an adequate sentence might be. Typically, they involved loss of numbers on the Navy's lineal list, admittedly not much of a tangible punishment if its only practical effect is to delay involuntary retirement for years of service beyond that point at which it would otherwise have occurred. Reduction in rank was available, but seldom used, and it suffered from the same shortcoming as loss of numbers in grade. Although dismissal from the service was a permitted sanction, the loss of pay and benefits to a retirement-eligible officer would have been severe. Perhaps if immediate involuntary retirement or separation with severance pay had been available these punishments might have been ordered in some cases. In the case of the *Missouri*, the captain, operations officer, and navigator were found guilty and sentenced to loss of numbers.

Whatever the shortcomings of the old Articles for the Government of the Navy, they still provided workable methods for dealing with professional error. The *Belknap* cases make it apparent that the general court-martial under the Uniform Code of Military Justice no longer offers a vehicle serving this purpose except in those almost nonexistent cases of willfulness or negligence so gross as to amount to reckless disregard. It must be kept in mind, of course, that there is still available a variety of lesser sanctions, some of them falling under the Uniform Code and some of them administrative. The essential question is whether this narrowed range is sufficient. If not, a substitute for the court-martial must be found.

Regardless of the answer to this question, the effectiveness of those sanctions still available should not be minimized. At the lowest level is the disgrace and loss of professional esteem inherent in the publicity given to the happening. This, while real and sometimes personally catastrophic, is more of a subconscious restraint than sanction. Next is the record of performance accumulated in an officer's fitness report file. It may ultimately result in failure of promotion and earlier separation from active duty, but its impact is usually widely separated from the event in time. Furthermore, in periods when the overall promotion opportunity is low, failure of selection will hit those with spotless records as well as those with unsatisfactory or unfavorable fitness reports. There, are, however, more immediate administrative sanctions, of which the most drastic is the summary removal from command. While an undeniably effective action, it almost always accompanies other sanctions in cases of major dereliction and may by itself be imposed for less serious breaches of standards. Examples would be unreasonable demands made upon his crew by an overzealous captain, or perhaps even a topless go-go dancer performing on the sail of a submarine. In the formal disciplinary area, the punitive letter of reprimand is undoubtedly the strongest action that can be taken short of the court-martial. When issued in conjunction with appropriate administrative sanctions, it is certainly sufficient to deal with the vast majority of untoward incidents that can befall a ship, such as dragging aground while anchored in bad weather, minor collisions, and various internal casualties.

But if the absolute responsibility of the captain for his ship is to be upheld, in cases of culpable inefficiency leading to major incidents, this lesser range of sanctions is not sufficient. A substitute for the general court-martial must be found. In the first place, all of the other actions may be taken against officers guilty of errors of judgment leading to less serious results. There seems to be little difference in the treatment of the commanding officer whose ship is severely damaged or lost and one whose ship is temporarily grounded or suffers a relatively minor collision. Perhaps as important is the loss of the collective judgment of a panel of disinterested professional peers. Although a letter of censure can be appealed one level, it is still essentially the action of a single senior in the chain of command. By the same token, exoneration by such a senior will have less impact than that by such a panel.

In the most serious cases the reaction outside the service must also be considered. It is questionable whether the public will accept what is primarily an administrative disposition in cases involving substantial loss of life or the loss of a major unit of the fleet. Removal from command and issuance of a letter of reprimand may be as devastating to the individual concerned as anything else that might conceivably be done to him, but the import of such actions is not understood by the public and is often perceived as a "slap on the wrist." Finally, where there is pressure for more drastic action, the Navy will probably be increasingly hesitant to resort to the court-martial, in view of the increasing emphasis being given to the concept of criminality in the evolution of the law applicable to court-martial proceedings. The Navy should properly be reluctant to stigmatize as a criminal an officer of the deck who was doing his level best to stay out of the way of a maneuvering aircraft carrier while attempting to perform the evolution in a manner consistent with what he understood to be the desires of his commanding officer. In this connection it should be noted that among the charges recommended by the investigating command to be brought against the *Belknap*'s officer of the deck was that of manslaughter. Fortunately, this charge was not included among those actually preferred.

An adequate substitute for the now practically unavailable court-martial in cases of errors in professional judgment need not have all the powers of such a court. It would not need the power to fine or imprison, and it certainly should not be deemed to have the power to impose criminal sanctions. It should, however, be empowered to exonerate and to impose sanctions with finality, subject to mitigation through appeal. Such appeal should extend to court review in the case of the most severe sanctions. The powers of such a tribunal should include the imposition of several levels of censure such as, possibly, a letter of caution, letter of admonition, and letter of reprimand—and extend in the most serious cases to the loss of the privilege of continuing in the profession. Separation from active duty, with or without severance pay, should certainly be included among the actions permitted. Dismissal of a retirement-eligible officer, while not entirely indefensible, is perhaps too drastic a power to give an administrative body. Lesser disqualifications should include revocation of formal designation of qualification in a warfare specialty or for command at sea.

None of the various techniques currently available to the Navy, administrative or judicial, can fulfill the requirements outlined above. A regular officer's right to tenure on the active list of the Navy is closely prescribed by statute, and therefore legislative authority would have to be obtained to establish any administrative body empowered to remove such an officer from active duty. It is certain that any approach which smacked of an attempted return to the general court-martial as it existed under the Articles for the Government of the Navy would never be acceptable to the Congress. However, there are other precedents, still in good standing, which have not only been established by legislative authority but have also been found constitutionally acceptable to the courts. Probably the professional licensing process, including revocation authority, as it exists under the regulation of various federal and state agencies, most closely parallels the administrative powers needed by the Navy as its chief method for the enforcement of professional standards through the use of sanctions. The Coast Guard regulates the licensing of merchant marine personnel. In cases of casualties involving merchant shipping, a Coast Guard board investigates, fixes blame, and can initiate action to suspend or revoke licenses. [. . .]

Whatever the precise details of such a system for assigning responsibility and enforcing professional accountability in specific cases, its essential elements are clear. Judgment should be by a panel of professional peers, enabled to act with finality, except for mitigation. The maximum sanctions available should be stern, including dismissal from the service. Finally, and just as important as the power to condemn, it must have the power to exonerate, to "fully and honorably acquit."

24 "DISCIPLINE AND THE PROFESSION OF NAVAL ARMS"

CAPT C. L. Bekkedahl, USN

How sharp a distinction should we draw between the Old Navy and the modern technological Navy? In a remarkable 1977 essay, a naval officer argues that the age of obedience compelled by the threat of punishment has passed, and the good order of contemporary military organizations should be created through forms of motivational technique that resemble those of civilian professions. The UCMJ, the author argues, is one of the kinds of military law that treats members of the armed forces as "wards of the state," a debilitating and outdated approach. This is not a thought that would ever have occurred to a nineteenth-century naval officer.

"DISCIPLINE AND THE PROFESSION OF NAVAL ARMS"

By CAPT C. L. Bekkedahl, USN, U.S. Naval Institute
Proceedings (May 1977): 186–201.

[...]

Our look at the past [. . .] identifies a number of significant aspects of naval discipline. By and large it was a harsh, inhumane, and wasteful regime, certainly in modern terms. It had the virtue of working in what was essentially an unsophisticated environment, mirroring a society not unlike itself, pursuing relatively simple goals: maintaining supremacy of command and exacting instant obedience from subordinates. Those in authority reinforced and sustained their authority by monopolizing professional knowledge. Reforms and changes to the forms of discipline took place over the years but these were slow to develop, stayed well within the standards accepted by society, and did not alter in any fundamental way the relation of the commander to the commanded. It took technology to do this. With the advent of steam propulsion and the myriad of other technological developments in naval warfare that poured forth, this change was accomplished first by sharing with, and then relinquishing to, the subordinates the bulk of detailed knowledge of the profession. The fundamental relationship was changed, and the form of discipline changed with it.

A look at today, then is really a measurement and appraisal in how far we've come in adjusting to the relationship and modifying the form of discipline to accord with reality. Most would agree that we are not very far along in this respect. We seem to have a foot in each camp and a sense that one or the other is going to have to be withdrawn. This sense of uncertainty has been with us for a long time and has been growing each year. Our ledgers overflow with specialized instructions and procedures on how to deal with one small element or another of interpersonal relations. People program after people program assails us for one purpose or the other, and the courts-martial system serves less and less purpose in terms of discipline. It costs enormous amounts of time, talent, and money, and when it does exact retribution for some offense, it is done in a vacuum, away from the crew, with no impact or example to justify its total effect. (At least flogging on the quarterdeck, because it was done before all hands, had the advantage of "encouraging the others.")

Pious pronouncements and exhortations to the contrary, our methods of getting the job done fall less and less often within the bounds of the chain of command or traditional senior-subordinate relations. We stagger along with arm-loads of so called benefits, incentives, rewards and restrictions, prohibitions and prescriptions, and it is doubtful whether anyone knows what they all are or why they were devised. We cling tenaciously to a rating system that is predicated on a concept, leadership, that is recognized as an anachronism (60 percent lead the remaining 40 percent?) and we try diligently to persuade ourselves that uniformity and consistency in the pay grade and rate structure are important, indeed overriding, considerations. The list of inconsistencies and *ad hoc* solutions in perpetuity that clutter our desks and heads is endless. Rather than continue the catalog it would be more useful to try and identify the underlying supposition that has produced this situation.

What price instant obedience? Once the central requirement of naval warfare, of this there can be no doubt. But, is it necessary today? The evidence continues to mount that the price of instant obedience is running higher and higher each day and that we may not be getting an acceptable return on our investment. In the days when a battle was decided alongside the enemy in hand-to-hand combat or in a point-blank cannon duel, then most assuredly a leader was well advised to have prepared his crew by conditioning them to unquestioning and rigid obedience. Instant obedience made it possible to sail crude and unsophisticated ships, survive the assaults of nature, control subordinates and discourage any challenge to authority, provide psychic gratification to those exacting obedience, and overcome the enemy in combat. Enormous resources of the military were devoted to exacting obedience from officers and men alike. The conditioning was formalized into working and living habits, and countless rituals and procedures were devised to extend this conditioning into every nook and cranny of life. These conditioning routines were stylized and passed down through the generations. But an erosion of their dominance began to appear as technology rose to the forefront. In our own times we have seen a drastic reduction of these routines that most recently were labeled "chicken regs" or "Mickey Mouse" by the former Chief of Naval Operations, Admiral E. R. Zumwalt.

Instant obedience certainly played a dominant role in the navies of yesteryear, and even though its preeminence has been eroded by technological advance, there is still an important place for it in the shipboard routine. Combat-sustained damage, fire, flooding, collision, and other material and life-threatening hazards are constant companions and will ever remain so aboard men of war. Only well prepared and carefully trained crews or specialty teams can assure survival in times of emergency. Instant obedience is a vital force in their conduct as anyone who has been to sea can vouchsafe. The key issue is whether instant obedience can be instilled by means other than the traditional conditioning regimens. There is a wide range of examples that can be drawn from hazardous civilian occupations that suggest it is possible, indeed desirable.

Perhaps the most pervasive feature of military life that requires critical examination in the technological era is that which is expressed by the term *in loco parentis*. The extent to which *in loco parentis*, in whole or part, permeates every aspect of the military is almost too difficult to grasp in its entirety: The officer or petty officer and "his men" (children?); their modes of compensation, health care, assignment of duty, food, clothing, training and education, working relations and conditions, punishment, reward, recognition, evaluation, separation, retirement, dependent care, allowances, and on and on. Is there any facet of the profession untouched by the hand of the substitute father? In days when it was either a ration of rum or a good flogging, when a man surrendered, voluntarily or otherwise, to the life at sea, then it could be understood that the system took responsibility and fulfilled the parental obligations. [. . .] More emphatically stated, the essence of professionalism is in total contradiction to the presumptions of this philosophy for the professional is one who, having examined, found worthy, and embraced the ethics and principles of a vocation, comports himself on the basis of self-discipline and internal rather than external directions and motivations. Herein lies the crux of the issue of naval discipline in the age of technological warfare. [. . .]

[. . .] More than anything else it is *in loco parentis*, and all it entails, which clouds and confuses our ability to nurture and promote a discipline of the profession. The forms of discipline embraced by it and those embraced by professionalism are not compatible with each other, and the large and growing force fields of contradiction between them are the heart of what we perceive as the problems of discipline in the military.

Consider: A methodology or reward and punishment designed to enforce behavior and reflexive, instant obedience, as much for its own sake as for the genuine requirements of the profession. We cannot avoid acknowledgment of the denial of professionalism inherent in the assumption that the members would do otherwise if given a choice, or fail to comprehend and accede, in circumstances requiring their instant obedience, i.e., in combat, fire, flooding and the other emergencies of one sort or another which occur in ships and aircraft. Hence, "always do as you're told or be punished, for this is the only way we can be sure you'll do the right thing at the critical moment." [. . .]

Consider: The body of special laws and regulations that apply to members of the military which, regardless of the efficacy at a given time or in a given situation, are all set in a context which says that military personnel are wards of the state, somehow either deserving of special treatment or incapable of conducting their affairs like their civilian counterparts, e.g., The Soldiers' and Sailors' Civil Relief Act, The Uniform Code of Military Justice, and similar executive orders or Department of Defense regulations.

Consider: The logic of the contractual system which binds the individual and the institution to each other and the complications which ensue when one is not suited to the other. The so-called enlistment contracts and rules governing a man's relationship with the profession are unique in our society and are distinguished by an unspoken but evident climate of mutual distrust. Were it not for the penalties the ingrates would run away.

Consider: The leadership and managerial philosophy that governs the relationships between personnel, leaders-subordinates, seniors-juniors, ranks-rates: It is a carefully nurtured class system. But, whatever virtues (never mind vices which are widely recognized) that a class system offers are then diluted by an almost paranoid devotion to the concept of consistency or to misguided notions of fairness. What remains is an inflexible structure that essentially denies obvious differences in intellect, talent, performance, and most important, the value of an individual's contribution to the achievement of the mission.

The foregoing are submitted as outgrowths of the concept of *in loco parentis* which in turn characterizes a major part of the form of discipline peculiar to the military. It is not suggested or implied that all these features are flawed or inappropriate or that the military and naval profession does not have its own set of circumstances that require special regimens, methodologies, or whatever. Nothing would be more misleading. On the other hand, the professionalism we seek is dependent upon development of the characteristics of self-discipline, open and inquiring minds, and self-sufficiency. It is dependent upon dedication to a work ethic and a life style reasonably akin to the thrust of the times. It is dependent upon those who would accept the hardships and risks inherent in the profession for the sense of purpose and satisfaction returned.

Is this revolutionary or alien to service life as it exists today?

25 "FREE SPEECH *V.* ARTICLE 88"

E. R. Fidell

During the Obama administration, a Marine Corps sergeant was administratively separated over the political content of a Facebook page he created and maintained, the Armed Forces Tea Party Patriots site. The debate over the limits of political speech for members of the armed forces is as old as the republic, and never fully resolved. Here, prominent scholar of military justice Eugene Fidell takes up the question.

"FREE SPEECH *V.* ARTICLE 88"

By E. R. Fidell, U.S. Naval Institute *Proceedings* (December 1998): 2.

Personnel in each of the armed forces have followed current developments concerning President Bill Clinton and *l'affaire* Lewinski with the same lively interest as other Americans. Recently, the opinions of several military officers concerning these events spilled into public view. An active-duty Marine Major wrote in the *Navy Times* that "one should call an adulterous liar exactly what he is—a criminal." Others circulated an e-mail petition seeking to drum up support for impeaching and removing the President.

In response, top leaders of the Marine Corps and the Air Force issued statements discouraging such efforts; in a memorandum, the Assistant Commandant of the Marine Corps said it is "unethical for individuals who wear the uniform of a Marine to engage in public dialogue on political and legal matters such as impeachment. Not only is it unethical, it could place the individual in violation of Article 88, Uniform Code of Military Justice." Inevitably, the press voiced concern about unlawful command influence over the military justice process in the major's case.

Because feelings are running so high, and also because these events reflect the tension between cherished constitutional values, it's important to go back to basics. [. . .]

The principle of civilian control does not restrict military officers from voting, contributing to political parties, or expressing personal views on vital issues of the day. It does, however, impose modest limits on political expression that do not apply to civilians under the First Amendment.

Article 88 of the Uniform Code of Military Justice provides:

> Any commissioned officer who uses contemptuous words against the President, the Vice President, Congress, the Secretary of Defense, the Secretary of a military department, the Secretary of Transportation, or the Governor or legislature of any State, Territory, Commonwealth, or possession in which he is on duty or present shall be punished as a court-martial may direct.

The *Manual for Courts-Martial* explains:

> It is immaterial whether the words are used against the official in an official or private capacity. If not personally contemptuous, adverse criticism of one of the officials or legislatures named in the article in the course of a political discussion, even though emphatically expressed, may not be charged as a violation of the article. Similarly, expressions

of opinion made in a purely private conversation should not ordinarily be charged. Giving broad circulation to a written publication containing contemptuous words of the kind made punishable by this article, or the utterance of contemptuous words of this kind in the presence of military subordinates, aggravates the offense. The truth or falsity of the statements is immaterial.

Violations of Article 88 strike at the heart of our system of government in ways that transcend the present controversy. They not only erode civilian control of the military but also threaten the hierarchical system *within* the military. Compliance with Article 88 is a baseline measure of obedience and loyalty; officers who violate it set a poor example.

It is a credit to the armed forces that officials rarely have resorted to Article 88. To be sure, from time to time issues have arisen under it and its predecessor provisions. There were numerous prosecutions during the Civil War, for example, President Lincoln having been deeply unpopular even among some Northerners. Since the Uniform Code of Military Justice took effect in 1951, there has been only one reported prosecution. In *United States v. Howe*, an Army Reserve second lieutenant was sentenced to be dismissed, to forfeit pay and allowances, and to be confined for a year for carrying a sign that said "LET'S HAVE MORE THAN A CHOICE BETWEEN PETTY FACISTS [*sic*] IN 1968" and "END JOHNSON'S FACIST [*sic*] AGRESSION [*sic*] IN VIET NAM." The United States Court of Military Appeals (now known as the United States Court of Appeals for the Armed Forces) had no difficulty upholding Article 88 against constitutional challenge.

Article 88 requires line-drawing. Subtle differences of language, tone, setting, and audience may put a case over the line. A quarter century ago, Army lawyers at Fort Monroe had to decide whether an officer violated Article 88 by displaying a bumper sticker that simply said "Impeach Nixon." They decided such a bumper sticker was not punishable. Other word choices might lead to a different outcome.

Some argue that Article 88 fails to provide fair notice as to precisely what is illegal. But vagueness is no stranger to military law, which punishes misconduct defined as vaguely as "conduct unbecoming an officer and a gentleman" or "conduct to the prejudice of good order and discipline." Yet few in uniform would throw these familiar concepts overboard.

There's ample room for the free expression of opinion in the military. Every branch has had its brilliant mavericks who have annoyed superiors no end even while contributing (in some cases significantly) to national defense. *Proceedings* itself, with its open forum that periodically causes heartburn for the management, is a continuing monument to free expression. But if Article 88 means the glass of free expression is not filled quite to the brim, this is so for very sound reasons which should not be forgotten . . . no matter how strongly one may feel on any particular issue of policy or politics.

26 "MILITARY JUSTICE?"

LtCol Gary Solis, USMC (Ret.)

The in-custody deaths of military detainees led to many controversies during the Iraq War. In an essay published during the height of the war in 2006, lawyer and former Marine Corps armor officer Gary Solis, the author of several important studies of courts-martial and military law, argued that the military justice system had failed to seriously address the deaths of Iraqis held by the American armed forces.

"MILITARY JUSTICE?"

By LtCol Gary Solis, USMC (Ret.), U.S. Naval Institute *Proceedings* (October 2006): 24–27.

Something odd is happening in courts-martial involving allegations of detainee abuse by American Soldiers and Marines. One takes no pleasure in noting that courts-martial in Iraq and Afghanistan seem to be acquitting individuals with unusual frequency. In courts that do convict, military juries sometimes appear unwilling to impose sentences commensurate with the crimes of which Soldiers and Marines have been convicted. "[D]espite strong evidence and convictions in some cases, only a small percentage resulted in punishments nearing those that civilian justice systems routinely impose for such crimes," the *Palm Beach Post* reported in October 2005.

By no means is it suggested that just because someone is charged they must be guilty. Every judge advocate has participated in courts-martial in which acquittal was probably the just result. And every conviction does not necessarily merit a heavy sentence. Nor should there be cookie-cutter sentencing. So one may presume that in each detainee abuse acquittal in Iraq and Afghanistan (and the United States), the accused was indeed not guilty. Perhaps the convictions and sentences that raise concern are isolated anomalies. But anomalous cases do turn up in press reports with some frequency.

For example, near Qaim, Iraq, in November 2003, Army Chief Warrant Officer Lewis Welshofer forced a badly beaten detainee with seven broken ribs—an Iraqi general—head-first into a sleeping bag, then sat on him and covered his mouth until the Iraqi was dead. (A defense witness, a pathologist, testified that the victim probably died of heart failure.) The homicide of a captive is a war crime—a violation of the law of armed conflict that, in the case of U.S. armed forces, is charged under the Uniform Code of Military Justice. CWO Welshofer was charged with murder and court-martialed. He was convicted of negligent homicide but sentenced to a surprisingly lenient letter of reprimand, a fine of $6,000, and two months restriction to Fort Carson, Colorado. No discharge, no brig time.

A co-accused chief warrant officer was also charged with murder. His charges were dropped in exchange for testimony against CWO Welshofer. CWO Welshofer's immediate superior, Major Jessica Voss, was granted immunity, as well.

In March 2005, Army 1st Lieutenant Jack Saville pleaded guilty to manslaughter after he and a sergeant first class forced three Iraqis to jump from a bridge into the Tigris River. One of the three allegedly drowned. Lieutenant Saville was convicted at court-martial and sentenced to a $12,000 fine and 45 days confinement.

Army Private First Class Willie V. Brand, 377th Military Police Company, was charged with the assault, maltreatment, and maiming of an Afghan detainee killed while in U.S. custody in Bagram. The victim was one of two Afghans found in the same cell, hanging with their hands chained above their heads, both beaten to death, according to their military death certificates. In August 2005, PFC Brand was convicted of all charges and sentenced to reduction in rank to private. No brig time, no discharge. A female co-accused, Sergeant Selena M. Salcedo, pleaded guilty to lesser charges and testified that before the victim died she repeatedly kicked him and repeatedly pulled him upright by his ears. She was sentenced to a one-grade demotion, a written reprimand, and a $1,000 fine.

In August 2004, Sergeant James P. Boland, from the same unit, was charged with assaulting one of the two murdered Afghanis just mentioned, "by shackling him in a standing position with hands suspended above shoulder level for a prolonged period of time." In June 2005, the sergeant received a letter of reprimand and was honorably discharged, without trial.

In September 2005, another soldier from the 377th Military Police Company, Sergeant Darin Broady, was tried for aggravated assault, maltreatment, and making a false official statement in the case of one of the two Afghani detainees he allegedly kicked to death. He was acquitted.

In June 2006, Private First Class Damien M. Corsetti, also charged with kicking and beating one of the two detainees, was acquitted.

Brig a Sometime Thing

These court-martial results notwithstanding, a dead body usually means substantial brig time for someone. But that often has not been the case. The troubled history of the Army Reserve's 377th Military Police Company includes 11 soldiers charged with prisoner abuse. Two homicides of detainees have never been charged. Of the 11 377th soldiers charged with abusing other prisoners, five courts-martial resulted in acquittals (one military panel deliberated for 15 minutes before returning a not guilty verdict), charges were dropped in three cases, one soldier was convicted but spared brig time, and two soldiers pleaded guilty. The unit's operations officer in charge of questioning the victims, Captain Carolyn M. Wood, was granted immunity and returned to Fort Bragg with the unit where she was awarded a Bronze Star. One might respond that it does not take long to acquit when there is no evidence. But there apparently was sufficient evidence for Army prosecutors and staff judge advocates—experienced senior military lawyers—to take these cases to trial. Perhaps the prosecutions were botched. Nine times.

In April 2005, in an unrelated case, Army Captain Roger Maynulet claimed his point-blank shooting of a badly wounded Iraqi who had attempted to run his roadblock was a "mercy killing." The captain was convicted of assault with intent to commit voluntary manslaughter. His sentence? Dismissal from the Army. No confinement was adjudged. Meanwhile, at Fort Campbell, Kentucky, at an April 2006 court-martial, Army Private Nicholas D. Mikel was sentenced to 25 years on conviction of attempted murder for shooting at a group of 22 fellow soldiers.

Vietnam Was Different

Sometimes, no charges at all are made. The Army investigated a special operations unit that, continuously for seven days, kept detainees "in cells so small that they could neither stand nor lie down, while interrogators played loud music" so they could not sleep. Some detainees were stripped, soaked, and then interrogated in air-conditioned rooms. One detainee apparently died from such treatment, the investigation found. The report recommended no disciplinary action, saying what was done was wrong but not deliberate abuse. In the case of the two Afghani detainees chained to the ceiling and beaten to death, Army investigators recommended that the NCO in charge of the interrogators, Staff Sergeant Steven W. Loring, be charged with assault, maltreatment, and dereliction. Instead, the staff sergeant left the Army, no charges ever having been filed.

"Well," one might argue, "we may not be seeing perfect justice in Iraq and Afghanistan but, hey, that's the way it's always been when our own guys are charged with war crimes." That would be incorrect. In Vietnam, 95 Soldiers and 27 Marines were convicted of the murder or manslaughter of Vietnamese noncombatants. The sentences imposed by Marine Corps court-martial panels were substantial, ranging from 10 to 50 years confinement and, in 15 of the 27 cases, confinement for life. Army sentences in Vietnam have not been researched but there is no reason to believe they were any less severe. But military panels in Iraq and Afghanistan sometimes take a different view.

In Iraq it is not only Army cases. Marine 2nd Lieutenant Ilario Pantano was charged with the April 2004 premeditated murder of two Iraqis apprehended at the scene of insurgent activity. At Lieutenant Pantano's pre-general court-martial Article 32 investigation ("the legal bullshit," as he put it) the lieutenant reportedly testified that he feared the two victims were about to attack him, so he shot them—up to 50 times, having to reload to do so. In his book, the lieutenant quotes his own interview on NBC's *Dateline*: "I shot them until they stopped moving." He then left a hand-written sign on the car against which the bodies lay: "No better friend, no worse enemy." The Article 32 investigating officer recommended charges not be preferred, and the case went no further.

When, on court-martial conviction, the punishment for killing a prisoner is restriction, a one-grade reduction, or 45 days confinement, what does that suggest about the attitudes military panels hold regarding the victims? What does it say about our commitment to military justice? Particularly when juxtaposed with 25 years for shooting at but not hitting American soldiers? No one would suggest that Iraqis and Afghanis are beneath the law's consideration because they are also insurgents. No one would contend that supporting our troops extends to insulating them from the consequences of battlefield criminal acts.

To be sure, in numerous cases the mistreatment or homicide of detainees have resulted in court-martial convictions and harsher sentences. Two soldiers convicted of the homicide of a female Iraqi interpreter received bad-conduct discharges and confinement for 18 months and three years, respectively. An Army staff sergeant was sentenced to three years confinement for the unpremeditated murder of a wounded 16-year-old Iraqi. A Marine received a year's confinement for using an electric transformer to make a detainee "dance." An Army private was sentenced to 25 years on conviction of killing a 17-year-old Iraqi male soldier after consensual sex. A specialist was sentenced to five years upon conviction of the unpremeditated murder of an Iraqi civilian noncombatant. Sentences to 25 years confinement, the longest imposed in Iraq, were handed down in two separate Army murder cases. The list of convictions, with sentences that might be anticipated, is considerable. But the cases that call into question the quality of military justice also constitute a disturbingly lengthy roster.

Command Responsibility

In the view of some, there is another problem as well. In March 2005, government reports released through the Freedom of Information Act (FOIA) said that eight prisoners who died in U.S. custody in Iraq and Afghanistan were homicide victims, fatally abused by their captors. Another Pentagon report, also released through FOIA in March 2005, said that 18 prisoners have died in American custody in Iraq and Afghanistan, apparent homicide victims. In February 2006, the *Philadelphia Inquirer* reported 34 suspected or confirmed detainee homicides since August 2002.

Retired Army Brigadier General David R. Irvine said that U.S. military officers were ultimately responsible for the actions of the soldiers under their command but that almost none had been held accountable, the *New York Times* reported in March 2005. As the general's statement suggests, the homicide of detainees too often raises the question of command responsibility. Every officer knows that the commander is responsible for everything that happens, or fails to happen, on his or her watch. But to rise to criminal culpability, the UCMJ adds that there must be some degree of personal knowledge or involvement on the part of the superior officer. In Iraq, the axiom of command responsibility has been conspicuous by its sometimes being disregarded.

FM 27–10, *The Law of Land Warfare*, paragraph 501, lays out the leader's responsibility:

> The commander is . . . responsible if he has actual knowledge, or should have knowledge . . . that troops . . . subject to his control are about to commit or have committed a war crime and he fails to take the necessary and reasonable steps to insure compliance with the law of war or to punish the violators. Examples of command responsibility overlooked: ten enlisted Soldiers have been convicted by courts-martial for their acts at Abu Ghraib. What officers have been court-martialed? Where were the watch officers? What was the commanding officer of Abu Ghraib doing all those nights? Who was the duty officer? Where was the adult supervision?

Army Lieutenant Colonel Steven L. Jordan, the ranking officer present at Abu Ghraib, has not been tried, and was only recently charged. Colonel Thomas M. Pappas, Lieutenant Colonel Jordan's Abu Ghraib superior and the commander of the interrogation task force, will never be court-martialed. At a non-judicial hearing, he received a letter of reprimand and an $8,000 fine. No court-martial, no possibility of brig time, no possibility of dismissal from the Army.

Brigadier General Janis Karpinski, who was in charge of Abu Ghraib when the mistreatment of detainees occurred, will never be tried. She was administratively reduced to the grade of colonel and given a letter of reprimand. But not court-martialed, not faced with the possibility of dismissal or confinement adjudged by a panel of her peers.

In an unrelated case, Captain Christopher M. Beiring commanded the Army's 377th Military Police Company in Bagram, Afghanistan. In December 2002, his soldiers, several of whom are referred to above, beat to death two Afghani detainees while they were chained to the ceilings of their cell. Captain Beiring, who trained and led the responsible soldiers, was charged with dereliction of duty and lying to investigators about his involvement. All charges were dropped; he received a letter of reprimand, and was released from active duty. (As already alluded to, four enlisted men in Captain Beiring's company were tried for the deaths of the two detainees. A sergeant and another soldier were acquitted; two pleaded guilty and were convicted of assault and maiming, not murder or manslaughter.)

Most of us are familiar with the grisly photo of the iced and plastic-wrapped dead body of Manadel al-Jamadi, who died at Abu Ghraib prison in November 2003, after allegedly being beaten by Navy SEALs. In May 2005, a SEAL, Lieutenant Andrew K. Ledford, was acquitted of beating Jamadi and also acquitted of failing to restrain his men from doing so.

Owning Up to Wrongdoing

In November 2004, Marine Major Clarke Paulus, who commanded Camp Whitehorse, Afghanistan, when a detainee was beaten to death there, pleaded guilty to dereliction of duty. At a general court-martial, he was found guilty and discharged from the Marine Corps, a Marine who did accept responsibility. Of the seven enlisted Marines involved in the actual homicide, only one went to trial. Sergeant Gary P. Pittman, charged with murder, was convicted of lesser charges and sentenced to reduction to private and 60 days restriction. No brig time, no discharge.

Pentagon statements that an officer's career is effectively ended by administrative punishment do not impress. The administratively punished officer does not face the specter of conviction by court-martial, hasn't the possibility of the dishonor of a federal conviction. He or she walks free while enlisted men and women for whom they were responsible sit in the brig, and the duty they failed to execute goes unmarked. And one could do worse than ending one's career as a colonel.

No commander is responsible for the unanticipated wrongful acts of subordinates. That is as it should be. But, as FM 27–10 specifies, if they knew or should have known of that misconduct, they bear responsibility for the wrongful acts of their subordinates.

Former U.S. Ambassador for War Crimes David Scheffer writes that cases like those mentioned

> reveal . . . disturbing weaknesses in the United States military justice system, including delayed investigations and remarkably light sentences. The deepest flaw is the failure to investigate and prosecute up the chain of command. . . . In recent years, our military courts pale in comparison with standards of compliance with the laws of war set by international criminal tribunals.

It has not always been so with military justice.

27 "THE CULTURE OF CHANGE IN MILITARY LAW"

(Selection from chapter 9 of *Evolving Military Justice*)

Eugene R. Fidell

The last word goes to a leading critic of the contemporary military justice system, a Yale Law School professor and former Coast Guard judge advocate.

"THE CULTURE OF CHANGE IN MILITARY LAW"

(Selection from chapter 9 by Eugene R. Fidell in *Evolving Military Justice*) edited by Eugene R. Fidell and Dwight H. Sullivan (Naval Institute Press, 2002): 163–68.

1.

Anyone tracing the path of military law over the last several decades will be struck by two phenomena: the extent of change that has overtaken the system . . . and the resistance to that change. Much of the change has been justified, or condemned, under the rubric of "civilianization"—the "*C* word," the mere utterance of which still makes the occasional senior military lawyer see red. A substantial body of literature has been produced in the process. But efforts to step back from the immediate issues of the day and consider the evolution of military justice in light of larger themes in the development of law and legal institutions have been rare indeed. With the lowering of voices that has characterized the stewardship of Chief Justice Robinson O. Everett on the United States Court of Military Appeals (and with fingers crossed that the court will be spared yet another spell of personnel and doctrinal turbulence), attention can usefully be turned to those larger themes.

2.

The received learning is that military justice is sui generis, springing from essentially different jurisprudential sources from those that gave rise to criminal and civil law. The Supreme Court has repeatedly sounded the theme that the military is of necessity a separate society with a correspondingly separate set of rules. The legislative basis of military law is also different from the bases of the other two bodies of American criminal law. Where else, after all, is the process of elaborating a code of criminal procedure left so overwhelmingly to the prerogative of the executive branch with so little involvement of the public, the bar, or Congress?

This description is unlikely to change in the foreseeable future. There are, however, other perspectives from which to consider the military and civilian legal systems. One of these—admittedly an elusive one—involves examining the process of change itself, and how those involved with the two systems view that process. On this level, the modern history of American military justice is essentially of a piece with the very *culture* of change in Anglo-American law over the last 150 years. This view is not at odds with the notion that military law sometimes serves different purposes from those served by general criminal law. It does, however, focus on an institutional dimension, which, if examined, may foster greater mutual understanding between the military and civilian bars. Such an improvement in mutual understanding is desirable as a matter of public policy in a democratic society committed to civilian control of the military.

3.

Time and again since the early nineteenth century, major changes have shaken the basic doctrines, institutions, and mind-set of the law here and in England.

Aspects of that history are instructive in thinking about the process of change in military law. In 1848 the New York Legislature enacted the Field Code, abolishing the distinctions between law and equity and radically altering one of the most fundamental aspects of the common law system. Influential as it was, both in other states and in Britain, the Field Code met resistance from distinguished members of the bench and bar in both countries. Referring to law and equity, for example, Judge Samuel Seldon of New York wrote in *Reubens v. Joel*: "It is possible to abolish the one or the other, but it is certainly not possible to abolish the distinction between them."

In his *History of American Law*, Lawrence M. Friedman wrote:

> Certainly the [Field Code] could not destroy the habits of a lifetime, nor, by itself, transform what may have been deeply embedded in a particular legal culture. But the stubbornness of the judges was a short-run phenomenon, to the extent it occurred. The real vice of the code probably lay in its weak empirical base. The draftsmen derived their basic principles from ideas of right reason, rather than from a careful study of what actually happened in American courts, and what functions and interests courts and their lawsuits served.

Professor Friedman also noted the effort of Dean Henry Ingersoll of the University of Tennessee, in 1 *Yale Law Journal* (1891), to decry the "attempt of one state to adapt a Code of Procedure prepared for an entirely different social and business condition." Addressing Dean Ingersoll's criticism of the adoption of the Field Code by North Carolina during Reconstruction, Friedman commented: "Actually, systems of procedure did not fit particular cultures so snugly. Ingersoll's diatribe mostly meant that code pleading was more easily attacked when it could be identified with an alien, and in this case, a hated culture."

To what extent is Dean Ingersoll's concern about the wholesale importation of concepts from one legal climate into another pertinent to the changes that have overtaken military law in our professional lifetimes? Respected observers have counseled caution in the adoption of civilian attitudes, and whether or not one agrees on any particular reform, that is certainly sage advice. Arguably there is a parallel between the gap that separated the New York that enacted the Field Code and the North Carolina that copied it, on the one hand, and the gap that separates civilian and military societies and defines their views of one another and of their respective legal systems, on the other. *Hatred* is certainly too strong a term for the relationship, but would *mutual distrust* do? Anyone who has practiced in both communities would have to acknowledge the accuracy of such a description. Worse yet, there is little prospect for bridging this gap so long as our society is content to treat the military as a separate society. "Out of sight, out of mind" seems to be the watchword. On the rare occasions when military justice is "in mind," the civilian mind—thanks in large part to the mass media, which fixate on the perceived outrage of the moment—can conjure up little more than stereotypes. [...]

6.

[...] The lesson to be drawn from the progress of law reform since the nineteenth century is one of patience and tolerance. We lawyers are a nostalgic lot. Symbolism and tradition count for much among us. As a result, it is important to take the longer view suggested by these historical analogies when addressing proposals for change and considering the resistance to change in military justice. The new should not be embraced merely because it is new. Nor should those who seek to preserve older approaches be derided as fuddy-duddies or worse for counseling caution or being loath to jettison institutions, modes of thought, and legal practices that they believe to be useful and legitimate and for which they view themselves as legatees and trustees.

Society ought to look to the custodians of military jurisprudence for professionalism. Professionalism, in a legal context, implies an unwillingness to accept circumstances simply because they exist if there is room for improvement in either substance or appearance. Appearance—symbolism—is critical in any system of justice. It is even more critical when the system in which the bulk of criminal defendants—often members of disadvantaged minorities—find themselves toward the bottom of an official totem pole, and typically have little if any say in the selection of their legal representatives, either at trial or on appeal.

Professionalism also implies creativity and leadership (a good military concept) in shaping and testing new approaches while at the same time being *appropriately* respectful of tradition, values, and empirically demonstrable special demands of the jurisdiction. Military lawyers must explore the meaning, as applied to them, of their duty as "public citizen[s]" to "seek improvement of the law, the administration of justice, and the quality of service rendered by the legal profession."

Military law is important to American society, and there is much that rightly sets it apart from the other sets of norms applied by the legal system. If a lawyer who uses his or her skills and energy to preserve the good and the practical in that system deserves praise, how much more so if those efforts are also informed by the lawyer's zeal for intelligent innovation where it is justified?

The old gospel song asks: "Will there be any stars in my crown when at evening the sun goeth down?" When the history of American military law is written, will there be any stars in *its* crown?

INDEX

ABOUT THE EDITOR

Chris Bray is a former infantry soldier and has a PhD in history from UCLA. He is the author of *Court-Martial: How Military Justice Has Shaped America from the Revolution to 9/11 and Beyond* (W. W. Norton, 2016).

The Naval Institute Press is the book-publishing arm of the U.S. Naval Institute, a private, nonprofit, membership society for sea service professionals and others who share an interest in naval and maritime affairs. Established in 1873 at the U.S. Naval Academy in Annapolis, Maryland, where its offices remain today, the Naval Institute has members worldwide.

Members of the Naval Institute support the education programs of the society and receive the influential monthly magazine *Proceedings* or the colorful bimonthly magazine *Naval History* and discounts on fine nautical prints and on ship and aircraft photos. They also have access to the transcripts of the Institute's Oral History Program and get discounted admission to any of the Institute-sponsored seminars offered around the country.

The Naval Institute's book-publishing program, begun in 1898 with basic guides to naval practices, has broadened its scope to include books of more general interest. Now the Naval Institute Press publishes about seventy titles each year, ranging from how-to books on boating and navigation to battle histories, biographies, ship and aircraft guides, and novels. Institute members receive significant discounts on the Press's more than eight hundred books in print.

Full-time students are eligible for special half-price membership rates. Life memberships are also available.

For a free catalog describing Naval Institute Press books currently available, and for further information about joining the U.S. Naval Institute, please write to:

Member Services
U.S. NAVAL INSTITUTE
291 Wood Road
Annapolis, MD 21402-5034
Telephone: (800) 233-8764
Fax: (410) 571-1703
Web address: www.usni.org